Sketch Map of

The

FINAL LINK

Great Western and

Great Central Railways

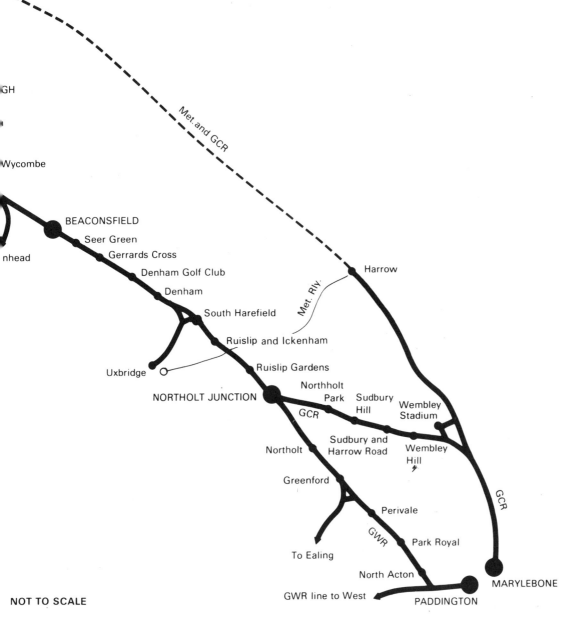

GH

Wycombe

nhead

BEACONSFIELD

Seer Green

Gerrards Cross

Denham Golf Club

Denham

South Harefield

Ruislip and Ickenham

Ruislip Gardens

Uxbridge

NORTHOLT JUNCTION

Northholt Park

Sudbury Hill

Wembley Stadium

GCR

Sudbury and Harrow Road

Wembley Hill

Northolt

Greenford

Perivale

GCR

To Ealing

GWR

Park Royal

North Acton

GWR line to West

PADDINGTON

MARYLEBONE

Met. and GCR

Met. Rly.

Harrow

NOT TO SCALE

The Final Link

The Final Link

A pictorial history of the Great Western & Great
Central Joint Line – the last main line steam railway
to be built in England and its effect upon the
Chilterns and South Midlands

Dennis F. Edwards & Ron Pigram

BLOOMSBURY BOOKS
LONDON

To Elizabeth Holkam Dell

who contributed so much to the typing
and final emergence of this book.

In the same illustrated series
Metro Memories by Dennis
Edwards & Ron Pigram
Romance of Metro-Land by Dennis
Edwards & Ron Pigram

This edition published 1988 by
Bloomsbury Books an imprint of
Godfrey Cave Associates Limited
42 Bloomsbury Street, London
WC1B 3QJ under license from Baton
Transport/Cleveland Press

© Dennis Edwards & Ron Pigram
1982

Design: David Morley-Clarke
Cover and map design by Vince
Power

ISBN 1 870630 017

Printed in Yugoslavia

The Authors
Dennis Edwards and Ron Pigram, in
their unique treatment of railway
history and social change, have
continued their research into the
railways that have affected the growth
of London and its countryside. *The
Final Link* tells a story that, as
practical historians, they have drawn
together from studies carried out for
lectures and papers given to a number
of societies in the south of England.

Dennis F. Edwards recently President
of the London Underground Railway
Society, and now Secretary of a West
London environment group, was born
in Middlesex, and is in many ways, a
product of the pattern of social history
which he captures in this series of
books.
As well as lecturing and producing
exhibitions on local history, he has
produced a number of leaflets and
booklets on the subject.

Ron Pigram has been involved in
railway history and the countryside for
most of his professional life. His father
worked for many years for the
Metropolitan & Great Central
authority. The Chilterns and Vale of
Aylesbury, through which this history
runs, is much loved and familiar to
him; sentiments that he distilled in his
very personal account *Around the
Historic Chilterns* (Midas) now out of
print. He is a Member of the Chartered
Institute of Transport. He also lectures
on many railway and social history
subjects. Walking, painting, and a
fascination with 18th-century
architecture provide his main
relaxations when not engaged upon
railway research — a subject both
authors describe as 'irresistible'.

Contents

Acknowledgements

The authors find it difficult to list everyone who, in small ways or large, or by their encouragement in the difficult early days of research work, have helped make this book a reality.

Thanks are due not only to the libraries and museums throughout the region covered by this book, but to dozens of private individuals who, without stint, have loaned, given illustrations or comment, or who have suggested avenues of effort. The librarians of Uxbridge, Brent and High Wycombe Libraries must be directly mentioned, as well as the practical encouragement from historians such as Charles E. Lee and H.V. Borley, who have set our feet firmly upon solid ground. Two people who have been very generous with their photographs have special mention: C.R.L. Coles and J.A. Fleming. Pictures have also been used from the excellent collection of work by S.W.A. Newton preserved at Leicester City Library. Jeff Levy helped with picture research.

We must also include Alan Fleck of the North Hertfordshire Museum, Kenneth Carr of Pamlin Prints, the Buckinghamshire County Museum, and Miss K. Day of Beaconsfield History Society.

The authors also wish to acknowledge the following sources of illustrations, with thanks:
C.R.L. Coles: Front Cover
Locomotive Publishing Company,
Oxford Publishing Company,
London Transport,
Leicestershire Museums, Art Galleries and Records Service,
William Fenton,
Science Museum, South Kensington,
High Wycombe Library service,
Buckinghamshire County Museum,
North Hertfordshire Libraries,
Illustrated London News,
H. Casserley,
London Borough of Ealing Libraries,
London Borough of Hillingdon (Uxbridge Library),
A. Fleming,
Miss K. Day,
Helen Hoare Collection,
Buckinghamshire County Council,
Charles E. Lee,
Pat Gadd,
Oxfordshire County Libraries,
M. Pope,
Robert Darlaston,
Pamlin Prints (Kenneth Carr),
Wembley History Society (Grange Museum),
Banbury Libraries,
Other photographs are from the authors' collections.

Foreword

Probably nowhere other than in the heady patriotic atmosphere of England in the dying years of the Victorian Age could such an expensive and unnecessary venture in railway building have taken place. Another link between London and Birmingham, that was to prove the very last steam main line railway built in England, had little sound financial logic in the dawn of the motor age. There was a Late Imperial flavour about the whole affair.

It was spawned by the powerful Great Western Railway's wish for a more direct line between London and Birmingham to gain additional traffic, and the Great Central Railway's difficulty in working high-speed trains into its new London terminus, via Aylesbury and Harrow, because of its argument with the Metropolitan Railway.

The Joint Line was to help the spread of London and to bring a promise of industry, as well as promoting trade in a very rural part of England. But these were the sunset years of Britain's great Railway Age. It was already too late . . .

The direct route from Paddington to Birmingham and the line from Marylebone to Grendon Underwood via High Wycombe was the last main railway line built in England. It was a route of 73¾ miles, of which 34 were owned jointly by the GWR and the GCR. The line was built for two purposes: The GWR wanted to shorten the mileage of its Birmingham expresses, which were facing competition from the LNWR (the new route would be only 110 miles as against 129 via Didcot and Oxford). The Great Central Railway needed an alternative route to the crowded and heavily graded line it shared with the Metropolitan via Quainton Road and Harrow to Marylebone.

The new railway was to open up the then remote countryside of the Vale of Aylesbury, as well as areas of the mid-Chilterns. It was also to develop the flat fields of West Middlesex for suburban and industrial development.

Yet as a main trunk line to the Midlands it had a life of only just over fifty years.

Built to the finest engineering standards, over-provided with large stations and goods yards, it was a case of arriving too late on the stage of railway history, and too inconvenient for the places it was designed to serve.

Yet despite Dr Beeching and later 'rationalisation', the main route of the Joint line survives. There are frequent trains from Marylebone to Banbury, and once a day it is still possible to travel direct from Birmingham to Paddington via High Wycombe – and back again in the evening!

This book tells of the background behind the building of the line; its subsequent effect on the economy of the places through which it passed. And through its pages we will go on a nostalgic journey from Paddington and Marylebone to Banbury – and on to Birmingham.

'The inauguration of the GWR/GCR
Joint Line of railway from Paddington,
through the Brent valley to High
Wycombe, has already accomplished a
great deal and will accomplish more in
the same direction, traversing as it does,
the ancient Perivale Forest and the uplands of Park Royal, and passing close to
Gerrards Cross and Beaconsfield.'
Rural London GWR 1924

'The opening of the line of railway
from Paddington to High Wycombe
has contributed largely towards
meeting the want which has grown
more and more intense since the
closing days of 1918, for it has opened
up a district of phenomenal beauty
which has somehow or other managed
to retain, not withstanding its nearness
to London, most of those old world
characteristics which have vanished
from more remote parts of the
country.'
*Leaflet issued by Great Western
Railway*

Middlesex
Gaily into Ruislip Gardens
Runs the red electric train,
With a thousand Ta's and Pardon's
Daintily alights Elaine;
Hurries down the concrete station
With a frown of concentration,
Out into the outskirt's edges
Where a few surviving hedges
Keep alive our lost Elysium –
    rural Middlesex again.
Sir John Betjeman

Perivale
Parish of enormous hayfields
Perivale stood all alone,
And from Greenford scent of
    mayfields
Most enticingly was blown
Over market gardens tidy,
Taverns for the bona-fide,
Cockney anglers, cockney shooters,
Murray Poshes, Lupin Pooters
Long in Kensal Green and Highgate
    silent under soot and stone.
Sir John Betjeman

Opposite.
A Great Central train for High Wycombe
leaving Marylebone about 1912.

Introduction

The Partnership

It was a happy ending to the great Victorian age of railways – a liaison between the venerable, yet forward-looking Great Western Railway ('The great awakening') and England's youngest railway which had fought its way from the north down to London: the Great Central.

The new route from Paddington to Birmingham and the links from Marylebone and from Ashendon to Grendon Underwood on the original Great Central was the final link – the last main line railway built in England.

This book starts at an age of success and of dreams, when the British Empire stood on its pinnacle and when railways were the pride of Britain, and the envy of the world. Especially, it is a record of the last link in a nationwide net of railways that had started with the first days of steam around Liverpool. The link had no high-sounding name; simply the Great Western and Great Central Joint Railway. It was built at a time when the railway building age had all but ended when the great army of navvies who had built the Great Central from the North via Aylesbury to Marylebone were about to be dispersed.

GWR Poster which summed up the railway's purpose.

10

Sir Edward Watkin
Chairman of the Manchester, Sheffield and Lincolnshire Railway (later Great Central), the South-Eastern Railway and, from 1872, Chairman of the Metropolitan Railway. It was his strategy to link the railways for the through rail route from the north of England to the coast. He retired in 1894, the year when the extension to London began, and his disappearance brought arguments between the MS & L and the Metropolitan Railways so that the London extension was not built in the way he intended.

Why did the Great Central need to build another line so quickly after the route of 1899, especially when its finances were not exactly healthy? What lay behind the Great Western's urge to push another main line to Birmingham, when it already had its old routes through Oxford, and when it had triumphs enough with the Severn Tunnel? Why choose to build through unpopulated country? To understand the reasoning of the day, and look at the countryside that the new railway served, it is necessary to examine the history of the Great Central and how it came to be built, before the *raison d'etre* for the Joint railway can appear. How did the London suburbs grow under the influence of the GWR and GCR? Why did some of the Buckinghamshire places flourish, whilst others failed to benefit by the new railway?

This book is a pictorial journey that begins at Paddington and Marylebone and takes you through the decade of Edwardian opulence; through the busy inter-war years and so to the highdays of the Post War years and the arrival of the diesel age.

The pictures come from a variety of sources, beginning with the remarkable collection of the late S.W. Newton, now held at Leicester Library, showing the construction of the Great Central and the Joint Line. His pictures depict for us the toil and the grandeur, the men, and the mechanical aids they used with such skill through the unyielding clay and chalk. Other photographs have seldom been seen before and come from local history collections, whilst others from the cameras of well-known railway photographers. It delves through the years of Stars, Kings and Castles, Directors, Robinsons, Thompsons, Westerns and the Blue Pullman to the present day.

The GCR line from Ashendon to Grendon Underwood (and beyond) may now be a sad trackway of weeds and grass; the great expresses may no longer run, but the Joint line is still busy with commuter traffic and there's still variety to be seen with freight trains and specials.

Setting the Stage

When Queen Victoria celebrated her Diamond Jubilee in 1897, most of the people in the great crowds on the London streets had got there by train, even from the remotest parts of the country. For by that period of the 19th century there were few towns and villages that were not within half a dozen miles from a railway.

Yet, oddly enough, one of the areas that was badly served was the central part of Buckinghamshire, as well as parts of west Middlesex, despite their nearness to London. For during the great age of railway expansion, only two main lines crossed the area – the London and North Western from Euston, and the Great Western from Paddington, both railway systems unlike the intricate web of lines that originated in Victoria, Waterloo and London Bridge. Thus the countryside adjacent to London on the north west side was not developed until the 1900s.

One of the reasons, it was said, was that heavy clay and lack of good water supply making the area unsuitable for building. But perhaps the real reason was one of economics. Those two early

The types that built the line.
Two studies of workmen of the 1890s. The farm labourers in this picturesque rural scene would probably not have thought of their lives as tranquil. The work was back-breaking, and there was little rest and very poor wages.

Better money was to be had by working on the new railway extensions – and the faces of these rugged navvies in the other picture tell all – again the hard work, but now a glint of humour in the eye.

In the general agricultural depression that swept England from the 1880s, there was relief with the coming of railway schemes, and a widespread movement from the land to this type of work resulted.

railway lines, the LNWR and the GWR saw their task as bringing the people and products of the North of England and the West Country to London. The possibility of carrying passengers from the villages and small towns on the capital's doorstep did not interest them. It was not considered lucrative. So places as near London as Perivale, Greenford and Ruislip, Uxbridge, Gerrards Cross and Beaconsfield remained undeveloped even by 1897. Some idea of just how remote some of these places were in the middle of the century is illustrated by the following extract from a book on the history of Ruislip by the Rev. John Roumieu in 1875: 'it would seem impossible to believe that such a quiet and secluded spot could exist within 15 miles of Hyde Park Corner; yet when it is remembered that no other place can be found in this radius so far from a station, our peace and retirement are easily accounted for, in our freedom from Sunday excursionists and all similar nuisances which fall the lot of easily accessible suburban parishes.' Going back even further, the poet Drayton wrote of rural and secluded Perivale in *Polyalbion* (1612):

'As Coln came on along, and
chanced to cast her eye
Upon that neighbouring hill where
Harrow stands so high
She Peryvale perceived pranked up
with wreaths of wheat.'

In the 17th century Buckinghamshire, away from the coach roads, was rural indeed. To this thickly beech-wooded land came John Milton to settle for a while at Chalfont St Giles and although he was by then blind, his verses recalled the days when he could remember waking up in the Chilterns:

'Sweet is the breath of morn, her
rising sweet
With charm of earliest birds;
pleasant the sun
When first on this delightful land he
spreads
His orient beams, on herb, tree, fruit
and flower.'
(*Paradise Lost* 641/47)

But there were disadvantages. Journeys to London were only for those whose work was with commerce. It was not unusual for carts carrying hay for the London market to set out from Ruislip and take 12 hours – for a return trip of 32 miles. The state of the roads – particularly in winter was a cause for concern right into the 1920s. In earlier times, places along the highways such as the Oxford Road were the haunts of highwaymen. Gerrards Cross got a bad name for this kind of activity and highwaymen were said to have 'flourished in wild luxuriance' on the bushy common. By the 1800s Gerrards Cross Common was noted for the richness of its blackberries, and people would make the journey on foot from

Great Central inspector's car.
This useful little vehicle was used by the railway inspectorate and surveyors working on the new railway. It seems to have been extremely difficult for the single operator to reach the perfunctory auto squeeze-horns that were the vehicle's only means of sounding its approach to workmen whose ears were tuned to the roar of steam.

13

Mission hut for children.
No religious aspect of the navvies' lives was overlooked as the men and their families progressed along the line of the new railway. The portable mission hut shown here must have had more attraction for the women and children than the hard-drinking navvies.

Uxbridge to gather the fruit. Henry Kingston described the hillside just above High Wycombe town in 1848, a few years before its branch line was built from Maidenhead: 'Sequestered little spot! Adorned by nature with many delightful variations of hill and dale, it seems to afford security for retirement, and for those who love to watch the sparkling brook and gaze with delight on the verdure and fertility of the surrounding pasture.'

Wycombe's growing chair making industry had to rely on horse drawn transport. One local poet recalled:

'Twas the month of May
From Wycombe we did start,
And Monday was the day,
When with our horse and cart,
We left our home to do our best
And with the Lord we left the rest.'

An old inhabitant of Beaconsfield recalled many years ago, the following description of the Uxbridge coach arriving: 'First you would hear the horn blaring out to warn of their approach. Then you would see the coach rounding the bend at the top of London End in a cloud of dust. At 'The Saracen's Head' four fresh horses would be waiting in the yard under the archway, and as the coach arrived they were led out – there was no delay; the weary steaming

arrivals were quickly unharnessed and the others took their places between the shafts. In no time, it seemed, they were on their way again to another long blast of the horn.

In his *Handbook to the Environs of London* (1876) James Thorn writes: of the flat fields around Perivale and Greenford: ' . . . good water is not readily available and the place has continued, therefore, to be left pretty much to the agriculturalist.'

By this time the once-famed wheatlands of Middlesex were being replaced by the more profitable grassland, which produced hay for London horses. The curate of Ruislip, the Rev. Roumieu comments again: 'The increasing demand for hay in London has slowly but surely brought about the extinction of arable land in its neighbourhood; and thus there remains but a few acres under cultivation at Ruislip . . . this change is certainly not at all beneficial to the poorer classes, whose employment during the winter months is much curtailed.'

In other words, there was much hardship in the countryside. In winter the country folk gathered firewood, which was taken to London by slow carts for sale. Others found employment in the great houses and their parklands. But, after the decline of the coach trade on the Oxford Road, places like Beaconsfield, West Wycombe and Princes Risborough lapsed into sleepy towns whose population was gradually seeping away.

This was the landscape, then, which existed until the later years of Queen Victoria's reign. Here's an example of how remote, even when the surveyors were marking out the new railway, a place like Gerrards Cross was from the pace of modern life: at the village school on the side of the Common one day the Headmaster announced: 'I have heard that a Motor car is to come along the Oxford Road this afternoon. If you behave yourselves, you may go across the Common and watch it go by.' Progress indeed was about to sweep across the Buckinghamshire countryside!

Uxbridge came on to the railway map at an early date, when the branch line from West Drayton was opened in 1856. But it was first at High Wycombe that the railway development that was later to play such an important part in the building of the Joint Line came about in 1854. On 1 August of that year the broad gauge Maidenhead and Wycombe line opened, reaching the town via the valley of the river Wye. The great Brunel is said to have been involved in the planning of the line in its early stages, including the extension to Princes Risborough and Thame in 1862. The coming of the line was greeted with cries of relief, particularly from the farming communities of Princes Risborough and Thame: 'It is said that our markets are not so flourishing as they were wont to be, the introduction of railways having directed the business greatly in other directions.'

The extension through the heart of the Chilterns was constructed 'as regards style and character and proportionate number of works materials and manner of execution, on the model of the Maidenhead and Wycombe Branch of the GWR'. In September 1859 a ceremonial start was made at Towersley between

Navvies resting near Wilton Park, Buckinghamshire.
Mugs of beer and hunks of bread-and-cheese serve as an impromptu meal for these navvies working on the construction of the GW and GC Joint Line in 1904. At this point, the railway runs through the Wilton Park estate, and the gentle slopes of the Chiltern Hills stand out clearly as a backcloth. Notice the 'pot boy' at the end of the row of men.

Making the way: The dramatic scoop through the chalk near Saunderton as the engineers work in the deep cutting to complete the 'up' line towards West Wycombe. This work was vital to allow high speed running, and the *Transport and Railroad Gazette* of 1905 remarked that to make gradients no steeper than 1 in 164, 'the new track passes through a long deep cutting and short tunnel in chalk, 65 feet below the surface'.

Risborough and Thame, when one of the directors cut the first sod and 'in a most workmanlike manner filled a wheelbarrow with which he walked the plank amid loud cheers, casting the contents some distance off the projected line'. The Wycombe, Risborough and Thame extension opened on 1 August 1862, the opening special consisting of three carriages filled with Directors and Shareholders. The locomotive was the somewhat old engine *Sunbeam* of the GWR's Sun class (1840). The service to London from Thame via Wycombe and Maidenhead took 2¾ hours and the fare, third class single, was 9 shillings (45p). In October 1864 the line opened through to Oxford. The year before another branch had been opened from Princes Risborough up to join the Aylesbury & Buckingham Railway at Aylesbury. The final line from Risborough was the Watlington branch which began operations in 1872. The Wycombe Railway was made standard gauge in 1870. But although some railway connections were thus established, there were still plenty of schemes being proposed. Here is a list of the main projects:

1845-6
The Aylesbury-Harrow-Greenford, Horsenden Hill and Wembley line, which would have linked with the LNWR.

1847
A line via Southall, Hayes, Ruislip, Chalfont, Beaconsfield and High Wycombe and possibly on to Aylesbury. The promoters of this scheme were the Uxbridge bankers, Hill, Smith & Co. Their prospectus stated that: the new line 'will attract traffic between the LNWR and the GWR lines in an area at present without railway accommodation'.

1853
The London and Mid-Western Railway, with a route from Oxford (where connections were to be made with the Oxford, Worcester and Wolverhampton Railway – the 'Old Worse and Worse', as it was called), to Princes Risborough, then High Wycombe, Uxbridge, Brentford (for the LNWR).

1861
The London, Buckinghamshire and West Midlands Junction Railway. This line would have had its London terminus in Sloane Square, although what the inhabitants of that salubrious neighbourhood would have felt, is best left to the imagination! The route to London would have been via Oxford, Thame, Princes Risborough, Amersham, Beaconsfield and in London, Addison Road (Kensington).

1864
The London and Rickmansworth, which would have started from the LNWR at Stonebridge Park and run via Alperton (with a branch to the GWR main line via Greenford), Roxeth, Pinner etc. It would have linked with a proposed Amersham and Chesham railway. Frederick Barry was to be its surveyor.

1865

The Harrow, London, Buckinghamshire and East Gloucestershire Railway. There was to be connections at Cheltenham for South Wales so that the coal traffic could be diverted from the GWR. The scheme was proposed by an Alperton businessman, Henry Haynes. However, it is possible that it was really sponsored by the Midland Railway.

1871

A line from the LNWR at Wembley running by way of Greenford, Ruislip (with a branch to Uxbridge) Gerrards Cross, Beaconsfield, Wycombe and across the Vale of Aylesbury.

1873

This was a revision of the 1871 plan, but a route that would have followed roughly that later taken by the Joint Line.

1885

A route to Beaconsfield and the Vale via LNWR at Willesden Junction, Alperton, Perivale, Northolt and Uxbridge. The surveyors were George Leane and William Bell.

1886

The scheme as 1885, but with the line running via Roxeth to Ruislip, with a branch to Ealing from Alperton. The promoter was Arthur Horne, who was Chairman of the Harrow Mount Estate. He obviously saw the line as a useful way of promoting his estate at Harrow Hill.

1895

The London and South Wales Railway by way of Ruislip, Beaconsfield, High Wycombe, Oxford and the upper Thames the LNWR, the Midland Railway and the GCR. It greatly annoyed the GWR who saw its coal traffic being diverted.

1897

The GWR promoted the Acton and High Wycombe Railway, Greenford Loop and Uxbridge Branch, 'in response to a scheme put forward by the Metropolitan District Railway'. The District wanted an Uxbridge and High Wycombe line with a route from Ealing and Roxeth. In the outcome the District scheme was cut short at Roxeth, the Metropolitan Railway stepping in with its own Harrow and Uxbridge Railway (Act of 1897). The Great Western secured powers to build its Acton-Wycombe lines.

1899

The incorporation of the Great Western & Great Central Joint Committee with powers to take over the Acton – Wycombe plans and to build Great Central lines from Neasden to Northolt Junction, and Ashendon Junction to the original Great Central line at Grendon Underwood, north of Aylesbury and Quainton Road.

In this way, the Joint line was born of many abortive schemes. It was also a remarkable alliance between two very dissimilar railways both in the way they were managed and the areas which they served.

The Strange Alliance

How did two such unlikely partners like the Great Western and the Great Central come to build the last great main line together? We must look back to the late 1880s, and to a provincial railway known as the Manchester, Sheffield & Lincolnshire which incorporated in 1846, during the height of the 'Railway Mania', and had built itself up into a sizeable concern. It planned to break away from its role of being just another northern railway and reach south to London. The railway was not a prosperous one (it had in fact gained itself the nickname of 'Money Sunk and Lost') but through the difficult country of the centre of England, it saw that it was still possible to drive a line that would be clear of congestion caused by established railways as they approached London. And through the line of an existing railway – the Metropolitan – it planned to pass through the busy London suburbs, already crossed by a maze of lines.

But plans are conceived by man, and a rather special force was propelling the Manchester concern southwards at a time when all reason cried out against such a belated attempt to fashion new railway empires. That force was Sir Edward Watkin, the son of a Manchester cotton merchant, and the Chairman of the MS & L since 1864. Watkin had been asked also to take the chair of London's ailing Metropolitan Railway in 1872, at its time of financial insecurity and disarray. He was in control of the South Eastern Railway, with its line from London to Dover by way of Folkestone. Watkin had an ambitious dream. But a dream that he kept to himself, for its magnitude and vision was strange, intoxicating, and heavy with problems. This dream was nothing less than a grand railway running from Manchester to Paris via a Channel Tunnel. It would, he realised, need a few more miles of track and a number of busy hours trying to talk the various railway shareholders into parting with money, but to such a down-to-earth brassy Victorian, it was certainly within his grasp. Sir Marc Brunel of all people, oddly enough, had unintentionally helped Watkin's idea when he built his tunnel under the Thames many years earlier. That tunnel had been taken over and developed as a railway tunnel by the East London railway, another of

Watkin's railways. The final fulfilment of the great dream of Sir Edward Watkin was a tunnel under the sea from Dover that would link Manchester directly in one long stretch of railway with France and all Europe. It was magnificent in its scope.

Watkin moved with great caution. The MS & L railway brought its lines southwards from a point near Sheffield to Annersley, a few miles south of Nottingham, where it made a connection with the Great Northern Railway. As far as the Metropolitan Railway was concerned, Watkin did not at first attempt to dazzle shareholders with bewildering prospects of a link-up with the Manchester concern. He did, however, hint that the Metropolitan carried goods traffic to only 4¾% of its total receipts, while on other railways the same traffic amounted to 50%. He dwelt darkly on the profits to be made north of London.

In the 1880s the Metropolitan railway crept steadily northwards to the Chilterns from Harrow, although on several occasions, Watkin even appeared to conceal the real purpose for extending the line, describing the rumours of a grand scheme on one occasion as a 'mere phantom of the imagination'. (General Meeting January 1886) In 1890, however, Watkin threw off his disguise and announced to the Metropolitan shareholders that he brought a 'valuable present': This was an agreement with the MS & L railway under which running powers were to be granted over the Metropolitan Railway from Quainton Road to Baker Street, a distance of 42 miles. The basis of profits was a division of 33⅓% traffic receipts to the MS & L railway, and 66⅔% to the Metropolitan. The idea was that the two companies would run their traffic into a magnificent joint station in London to be built at Baker Street, on the way to Dover.

In spite of Watkin's assurance to the shareholders that there would be established 'a great road to London out of which there would be a resulting profit that would startle some of your expectations', the Manchester company increasingly had an uneasy feeling that it had by no means obtained the best of the bargain, and tried by agreement to raise the percentage of receipts over the section to 50%. When this attempt to amend the agreement proved fruitless, the MS & L tried to prove that the Metropolitan Company was incapable of carrying out the agreement because of the congestion of traffic on its line caused by the 'success' of the Metropolitan's Wembley Tower:

Steam Power and Muscle
This machine has a full covering of corrugated iron sheeting to protect the crew from the weather and from falls of material.

All the nearby construction men have been gathered for this apparently official picture, so the excavator may well be one of the company's best. It was at work on the construction of the Joint Line near Wilton Park, Beaconsfield in 1904.

Wembley Hill
Digging into the London clay wasn't easy, especially when it was high summer drought, or mid winter floods! But in 1901/02 there were mechanical steam shovels to help with the worst of the task. Clearly seen here is the rather sinister half finished bulk of 'Watkin's Folly' from which one could gaze over the valley of the sparkling River Brent to London's outskirts at Willesden Green!

Near the Tower
Navvies resting during the construction work near Wembley Hill. The steel structure in the background is the first (and only) stage of the ill-fated Tower scheme of the Metropolitan Railway Company – The Tower was known as 'Watkin's Folly'.

Watkin's Folly
The remaining 'leg' of Watkin's Tower
before its demolition in 1907.

'The accommodation between
Wembley Park and London provided
by your Act is insufficient, and the
necesssity for an independent running
line to London is most urgent when the
crowded state of your present system at
holiday and at other times is taken into
consideration, and a separate line from
Wembley Park is indispensable' the
MS & L argument went.

This resulted in the Metropolitan
being forced to agree to construct for
the MS & L a separate line running
beside the original lines.

The Wembley Tower just mentioned
formed the centre of the argument. It
was a frivolous whim of Watkin who
had been impressed by the success of
the Eiffel Tower in Paris, which had
repaid the whole cost of its
construction, £780,000, within seven
months. In due course the
Metropolitan's offshoot company had
begun a structure of sorts that began to
take shape at a spot now the centre of
Wembley stadium. It failed to reach
higher than one storey, and became
known as 'Watkin's Folly'. In only a
few years even the Metropolitan knew
the Tower to be a complete failure, and
John Bell, who had replaced Watkin as
Chairman of the Metropolitan Railway,
stated in September 1894 that the
'resources of the Tower Company are
now exhausted'.

From these years arose the bitterness
between the two main links of Watkin's
great Route to Europe, and the weight
of the double failure of the Tower and
the destruction of the Trunk Line
scheme fell upon Watkin himself. By
July 1895 the MS & L railway
successfully planned the separate line
to run alongside the Metropolitan

railway nearer London and establish its
own London terminus at Marylebone,
'ploughing a way through the best
residential part of St John's Wood to
their station in the Marylebone Road',
with detrimental consequences to the
Met's traffic.

In November 1894, in a rash of
steam excavators, work started on the
extension of the Manchester, Sheffield
& Lincolnshire railway's new extension
into London, with a Northern Division
responsible from Annersley Junction to
Rugby and a Southern Division from
Rugby to Quainton Road where the
MS & L railway (which was to be
renamed the Great Central), met the
line of the Metropolitan Railway at
Quainton Road.

A Metropolitan division of
construction was formed to carry the
Great Central railway from the
widened lines of the Met at Canfield
Gardens, Hampstead, to the new
London terminus at Marylebone, a
distance of 1 mile 71 ch.

Only six months earlier, Sir Edward
Watkin resigned his place on the
Metropolitan Board and John Bell
(who once had been an apprentice with
the MS & L railway) took his place. In
those early days Bell had been in close
contact with William Pollitt, who was
also employed by the MS & L railway.
Pollitt had become General Manager of
the northern concern, but the two men
were violently hostile to each other, a
fact that finally was to prove the
catalyst for the creation of England's
last Main Line.

A climax between the two men
finally arose in July 1898 when the
Line into Marylebone had just been
completed. On the 25 July 1898 coal

trains began to rumble over the new railway to iron out and consolidate the road, and five days later, on 30 July, the Great Central Railway, claiming that it was entitled by a Licence granted by the Metropolitan Railway to run traffic on to the Great Western Railway's line at Aylesbury, signified that it intended to dispatch the first train over the Western's route on that day. Bell was furious, and rushed in the middle of the night to the spot north of Quainton Road Station, with a band of 'volunteers' to halt the goods train, setting the blocking signal with his own hands.

Bell was in the signal box in time to see the Great Central train, which hove into sight above 3.00 am, stop at the

home signal that he had personally set against it. Bell told the astonished trainmen that it was not going to use 'his' railway until matters between him and the General Manager were settled. There was nothing to do but to wait for another locomotive to come from the north, as it was impossible to propel the heavy coal train backwards.

The result of Bell's astonishing manoeuvre was to rebound heavily against the Met. The Great Central was determined to have no further interference and went into partnership with the Great Western Railway for a new Joint route to London via Princes Risborough and High Wycombe. The Great Central Act of 1898 had sanctioned a line between Neasden

The Great Central Bridge over the Regent's Canal
One of the major engineering feats of the London extension.

A temporary 'coffer dam' was constructed to allow the necessary piling to take place. It was formed by timber sheet piling, with clay puddle very appropriately used between the rows of board to arrest the seepage of canal water. This made a very effective dam, and only a small amount of water had to be dealt with by pumps.

Box girder bridge and tunnels: St John's Wood
The construction of the cut-and-cover tunnels here was one of the most interesting parts of the contract for the Great Central's London-bound extension. Heavy plate main box girders were used to cover the 90-foot span to carry Lodge Road over the railway, near this site. The surviving buildings in this scene at Alexandra Road have been supported and the underpinning of these structures near the line was so difficult that special miners were used, working only for strictly regulated periods at a time.

Marylebone:
Twin tunnels proved to be far too generous and in the end only one was laid with double tracks for the Great Central trains. The buildings above the tunnel have just been rebuilt and the surrounding streets are getting back to normal.

Cut and cover work
The six-ring structure of brickwork can be seen in this view of the cut-and-cover tunnel work used on the Great Central's extension into Marylebone.

(where the company had its new depot) to Northolt Junction (later called South Ruislip); within a few weeks of Bell's interference, the Great Central and the Great Western railways agreed to construct a line from Northolt to High Wycombe, improve and double the existing single track of the Wycombe Railway from there to Princes Risborough, and to build a double line to connect with the Great Central main line at Grendon Underwood, well clear of the Metropolitan at Quainton Road. The Bill was introduced to Parliament in 1899, and was duly passed. So began the final chapter in the great age of English Railway construction.

When the Metropolitan Board realised the full horror of what the Great Central and the Great Western

planned to do, it decided to lodge a claim for loss of traffic at once, for the new Joint Line was to run clear of the Metropolitan at every point – via Grendon Underwood, Princes Risborough and Ruislip into Marylebone. The complete loss of all Great Central traffic, estimated at £74,000 in a year, would have been a catastrophic collapse in traffic receipts. Moreover, everybody saw that the new Joint Line would be a better one, taking the fast expresses clear of the worst problems of the Chiltern Hills over which the Metropolitan ran. It would avoid the tight curves and heavy gradients and offer to the fickle Edwardian public, over-provided with train services, the advantage of fast new express trains – something that it

Marylebone station
The Great Central spent so much money getting to London that its finances were rather the worse for wear by the time the site of Blandford and Harewood Squares were cleared in London for the goods yards and terminus. So the buildings were a little less grand than perhaps Sir Edward Watkin had originally dreamed. The goods yards and coal depots were built on a 51-acre site. Sir Douglas and Francis Fox were the engineers for the two miles of approach tunnels to Marylebone.

Marylebone station under construction
The terminus of the Great Central Railway and the London end of the new Joint line with the GWR was planned with future expansion in mind. During the construction of the nearby goods depot, it was necessary to underpin the end wall of the nearby 'Nightingale' public house. The workmen digging these foundations were known to be a secretive bunch, but the reason for this was soon to appear when the landlord was heard to declare that many cases of his best ale and wines had vanished from his cellars on the far side of the wall. Of course, all the evidence had 'disappeared' when the mystery was investigated!

had to do if it was to stand any chance of winning traffic from the established companies.

However, the Great Central people realised, also, that the new Line via Princes Risborough would take five years to build, and it was essential that the Great Central, whose capital had almost run out on a number of occasions on the way to London, started to gain repayment for money which the London extension had cost.

It was with relief, therefore, that the Met's negotiating team of Lord Aberconway, Sir William Birt and Colonel J.J. Mellor found the Great Central prepared to play ball, after it seemed to hold all the trump cards. The collapse of the Metropolitan could be averted! The Great Central had

received a claim for proposed loss of traffic, but the Met realised that pure monetary compensation would have left it with certain lines that it would be prevented from using. The mission of Lord Aberconway, therefore, had been to get the Great Central to agree to continue to use the original Joint Line through Aylesbury after the rival Joint Line with the Great Western was built. The final agreement was that the Great Central would lease the separate line built for it by the Metropolitan to Harrow South and for the Great Central to own jointly the railway to Verney Junction. In this way the new Great Central Railway had a choice of ways into London, while steady traffic started to use the Joint Line with the Metropolitan Railway.

Marylebone

The building of the Great Central Hotel, designed by Col. Robert William Edis. The building was made of hard pink Midland bricks, with yellow terra-cotta dressings (supplied by Doulton) and the architecture was in the Flemish Renaissance style. The brickwork was of the highest standard and only the best craftsmen were taken on. For their refreshment, beer was carried around to the bricklayers in pint cans with handles threaded to long poles, a practice that was quickly to disappear for ever.

The interior fittings described on the notice board high up on the building, were by Sir Blundell Maple. Up on the roof a cycle track was installed – although it may have been more of an entertainment than a serious move to reduce the corpulence of the hotel's northern patrons.

Sir John Betjeman has described the hotel and the station (opened on 1 July 1899) as 'A public library which has unexpectedly found itself in London'.

The New Terminus at Marylebone

One morning in 1897 a patrolling security man keeping an eye on the tip wagons had rather a shock when he looked at the large steel box girders that stretched the 90 ft span of the railway carrying Lodge Road over the new lines south of St Johns' Wood, for the slumped figure of a man could be seen inside the actual girders. The man was quite naked, and was lucky to be alive. He claimed to have spent the previous evening on a drinking spree in the West End and had fallen into a stupor. Someone had seen him, had taken him in a cab to a dwelling near the railway, and after stripping him of his possessions and clothes had dumped his body inside the box girder.

This tale was one of many strange stories about the building of the short extension line into Marylebone Station. From May 1896 to July 1898 13 locomotives, 6 portable engines and 'steam-navvies' helped the men at work on the solid London clay. It was a vast task, and tunnelling went on day and night with a pause only on Sundays. The Act under which the railway was being built forbade the use of the local streets to transport spoil and up to 13 trains a day, hauled by Metropolitan engines, dragged the stuff out to Neasden.

Decauville narrow-gauge rail track and tilt waggons were used for immediate spoil. Here was the setting for another mystery; workmen arrived at work early one Monday morning to discover a bloodstained cap and splashes of blood at the bottom of a trench by the railway boundary wall. A youth had climbed the wall on the Sunday and had been skylarking with some of the light waggons. The one on which he rode had tipped over and had crashed down, taking him to the bottom of the trench. Presumably he had managed to drag himself off before dying of his injuries.

The main works at Marylebone consisted of the construction of the passenger and goods station, several bridges including one over the Regents Canal, three tunnels under Lords Cricket Ground, heavy egg-shaped

brick tunnels between Wellington Road and Finchley Road and some major underpinning works. It was a formidable task. A vast area of property at the site of the works had to be demolished; Harewood Square completely disappeared, and Lord Portman, the owner of the property, claimed £400,000 for compensation from the railway for alleged depreciation in value of the remaining houses because of the railway terminus. He was awarded £250,000. Portman's claim was typical of the attitude of property owners who regarded the railway as fair game.

Thousands of the bricks from these demolitions were cleaned by piecework labour and re-used as backing bricks for the heavy retaining walls that were built with stolid caution near the tunnels. Much of the hard brick ends were crushed mechanically and mixed with ballast to form a rock-hard concrete. Five huge blocks of dwellings were built before the demolitions to house those people displaced; they were called 'Wharncliffe Gardens' after

Lord Wharncliffe, the Chairman of the Great Central.

There was a big demand for bricklayers, and first-class men were paid at the high rate of 10d (4½p) an hour. Anybody brazen enough to claim full knowledge of bricklaying was certain to get a job, although the quality of the brickwork was excellent. Bricklaying was thirsty work; beer boys. specially employed, carried beer around in pint cans with handles threaded on long poles. Carpenters were employed at 9d (4p) an hour. Keymen and scaffolders received 7d (3p) an hour and the ordinary navvy got just a 1d less. Work proceeded furiously; so quickly in fact that the supply of bricks ran out at times.

The whole of Marylebone Station was 'made ground', so it was necessary to dig out to about 20 feet to get satisfactory foundations in the virgin soil. Nobody wanted to waste such a useful space, so that in due course the excavated area became cellars for the Refreshment department and was filled with various casks and bottles.

Accident prevention
The arrival of GCR in London was marked for a time by a change in coaching livery to dark brown with grey upper panels. The first passenger train on the new London extension ran on 15 March 1899 and six years later the joint GW and GC line was opened. The coaching stock was of a generally higher standard than most other London stock of the time, and the heavy Dreadnought coaches had anti-telescoping blocks at the end of the carriages to keep them in line in case of accident.

Between the tunnels near Lords Cricket Ground, on the open section alongside Wellington Road, the most massive of the retaining walls appeared. The brickwork here stood solid, on a 14 foot base, and the walls reached up to a height of 35 feet. Even then, they were thought not powerful enough and concrete feet were added later because the clay here was judged to be treacherous by Rowlandson, the Chief Engineer of Sir Douglas Fox and Partners, Engineers for the Contract.

The construction of the egg-shaped tunnels over this section of railway leaned heavily upon the skill of the tunnel miners. The tunnels were constructed to the 'bottom heading' method. This heading was large enough to take ordinary low-sided railway waggons and special contractors' waggons hauled by a locomotive with a dwarf funnel. Timbering was with main crown bars of 18 inches diameter larch, with 12-inch pitchpine logs to form the main raking struts. The only time when these caverns of gloom were free from the attack of the navvies was on Sundays, an ideal time for the locals to pry into the workings.

The warehouse at Marylebone, which was destroyed in the Second World War providing 6,000 tons of steel for the war effort, was a source of great wonder at the time. Although this seems to have missed the probing camera eye and the attention of Mr Newton, this structure, under the main contractors, Firbank, had a basement and ground floor designed to take railway trucks, and lifts to connect with the five other floors for storage of goods. It was the largest in the country and with the other buildings cost the best part of £1,300,000.

One of the features of the contract was the widening of the Regent's canal – a task then carried out with two rows of timbers to form a coffer dam. Between the wood clay puddle was forced, making an effective barrier that was easily controlled with pumps. Heavy machinery was transported to the site by barge, and a 40-ton Goliath Crane swung the material on to the site.

By July 1898, the great edifice of Marylebone and its shining new lines lay virtually complete in the sunshine, although piles of builders' spoil and barrows stood everywhere. Some of the more prosperous of the engineers took themselves off for a champagne dinner at the Holborn restaurant, then on to a show at the Alhambra at Leicester Square, and on to a round of late drinks at 'Jimmy's' in Regent Street before taking a hansom cab back to Baker Street. For the Directors, a more grand opening celebration of the great enterprise lay ahead.

Arrival of the local beer
The brewer's horse-drawn dray brings fresh supplies of beer – almost a daily necessity for thirsty workers of the rural communities of the Chilterns.

This picture was taken in 1903 outside 'The Swan' at West Wycombe, an inn that sold Wheeler's beer – a local High Wycombe firm.

The two-horse 24-seater bus made a regular run from West Wycombe to Loudwater and was owned by the Livery & Posting Company.

Watching the British workman
Officials watching a line of navvies at work, outside the old High Wycombe Steam Laundries, preparing the ground for the new Joint Line tracks, 1902.

Steam cutters at work
Railway construction had been rapidly increased by the use of steam excavators. In a rather shallow cutting, the steam cutters (in one case 'improved' by the operators by the addition of rough sheeting) is in the process of depositing a scoop of chalk into a waiting horse-drawn rail truck, while on another constructors' line a fresh supply of coal for the digger has been brought up. The sides of the cutting are already being smoothed by navvies with pick-axes. These works near Princes Risborough were for the Saunderton 'cut-off' line.

High Wycombe

This is how Pauling & Co. built the high embankment near High Wycombe at Loudwater. The archway on the right is part of Sir Philip Rose's Viaduct.

The locomotive is probably Class K 'Beaconsfield', No. 58, built by Manning Wardle in 1902. Sir Philip owned the land here and insisted that the viaduct was built of red bricks to blend with the landscape.

Notice Board

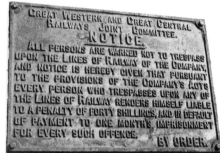

Through the chalk

The majestic sweep of the Chilterns, crowned with their beech woods is unspoiled as yet by motor traffic. This was the background when the work began on the new 'up' line between Princes Risborough and Saunderton.

The work included a 88-yard-long tunnel and these very deep cuttings. But it was all worth it to reduce the gradient for Paddington bound trains. The original route of the Wycombe Railway became the 'down' line and was situated to the west of the new formation.

Princes Risborough, 1890

A little Chilterns town that, before the new railway arrived, had slept away the long hot afternoon of England's imperial age served only by remote rural trains. It was to become a junction for the GW and GC main line from London, and for services to Oxford, Aylesbury and Watlington.

This is a view of the High Street taken from the Market Place in 1890 as part of a County record for the Royal Commission. It shows a ghost town, unpeopled by children with only the grotesque top-hatted figure of the local tailor looking from his doorway on the right, while the cameraman's horse and dog cart await his return with placid indifference.

Thame market

In this old print of this little country market within a few miles of Princes Risborough, the cattle are tethered in small groups along the length of the main street. There was considerable livestock movement by railways serving the Vale of Aylesbury and the surrounding areas into London.

Local butchers had their own slaughter-houses, often adjacent to their shops where the cattle died with great suffering. A boy from a village under the scarp of the Chiltern Hills recalled later: 'Some butchers were not particular in closing their doors and in common with other children, my brothers and I witnessed all the processes incidental to the creation of chops and steaks. Repulsive and improper many will say, but after all, it taught us the truth about a sad feature of our civilisation.'

Building The Line

Work on the new line agreed by the Great Western and Great Central Railways after Bell's interference began in 1901, the resident engineer for the GWR being R.C. Sikes. The first six miles or so of the GWR section to Northolt Junction left the original GWR line at Royal Oak Common and passed through North Acton, Park Royal, Perivale, Greenford and Northolt. The contractors were the Westminster firm of Pauling and Co. Limited.

The work proceeded at a good pace and on 15 June 1903 the first passenger service was run in connection with the Royal Agricultural Show at Park Royal. The trains took the new line to the junction south of Greenford, then down a new connecting line to West Ealing. Between Northolt Junction, where the Great Central's spur from Neasden was joined, the line to High Wycombe was built once again by Pauling and Co., under a contract worth £580,000. The GWR appointed J.C. Inglis as Engineer, with Mr Sikes as resident engineer. Further north, the Great Central agreed to build an 8-mile branch from Brackley down to Banbury so that it could run its coal trains to the west and the south. On the route to High Wycombe from Northolt the work was divided into sections, each with a manager. Mr O'Connor was responsible for the Northolt Junction to Denham section; Thomas H. Davies, Gerrards Cross-Denham-Uxbridge; R.J.B. Sharpe for Gerrards Cross to High Wycombe. The work force numbered 2000 men, and they were well equipped with all the latest civil engineering aids of the day, including 12 steam navvies (mostly supplied by Rushton and Proctor). There was a stable of 29 steam locomotives, 500 tipper wagons, 100 trucks and 50 horses. Over 30 miles of standard gauge light railway track was laid (using 60lb rails) to carry away excavated soil and to supply constructional materials, as well as providing workers' transport to the more distant parts of the workings.

Paulings established a main depot at Gerrards Cross with accommodation huts for the men, a mission hall, medical centre and recreational facilities, as well as 'attractive bungalows' for the superintendents. There was also a depot and repair facilities for the locomotives, which included five of the classic 'Terrier' tank engines purchased in 1902 from the London, Brighton & South Coast Railway.

They were:

No. 36 Bramley	Worked in 1890s on West Croydon-Wimbledon line.
No. 39 Denmark	Scrapped about 1909.
No. 49 Bishopsgate	Scrapped about 1909.
No. 52 Surrey	She was later believed to have gone to La Plata Tramway in South America.
No. 57 Thames	Also sold to La Plata.

The other locomotives used in the construction work included:

Makers	Works Number and name		Place known to have worked
Hudswell Clarke	75	Sam	Princes Risborough
ditto	444	Haddenham	Haddenham
ditto	650	Birkenhead	Haddenham
Hunslett	188	Willie	Denham
ditto	464	Palacios	Gerrards Cross
ditto	454	Norman	Haddenham
Manning Wardle	713	Punch	High Wycombe
ditto	1518	Liverpool	Haddenham
ditto	205	Preston	Wotton
ditto	620	Helen	Saunderton
ditto	1112	Pellon	Denham
ditto	1145	Number 15	Wembley Hill
ditto	1232	Dunragit	Gerrards Cross
ditto	1535	Beaconsfield No.58	Gerrards Cross
ditto	56	Northolt	Ruislip
ditto	1539	Penn No.60	Denham
ditto	1541	Gerrards Cross	Ruislip
ditto	1378	Peterhead	Haddenham
ditto	1542	Denham No.61	Denham

Paulings also had depots for the locomotives at Northolt, Ruislip and Ickenham and at High Wycombe. Most of the engines were fitted with wheel washing equipment, a necessary device with the wet winters in the Middlesex clay and the sticky Chiltern chalk.

The Great Central's line from Neasden to Northolt Junction was commenced in November 1901. The contractors were Thomas Oliver and Sons of Rugby. Pattinson and Son of Westminster built the stations.

The line was to cost more than the original estimate, because of the extensive excavation works at Wembley Hill, and on the southern edge of Harrow Hill at Sudbury Hill. The estimate in 1898 had been £168,200, but the final cost came to a staggering £300,000.

The Wembley Hill work had originally been planned as a tunnel, but the engineer decided that a deep cutting would be cheaper. Nearly a mile of heavy Middlesex clay – some 640,000 cubic yards had to be removed during the winter of 1904/05, in places to a depth of 60 feet. A 30 foot high and 158 foot long retaining wall was built along the foot of the hill.

Unfortunately, on 18 July 1918 there was a major landslide here. In about 30 minutes the slope moved, pushing the wall about 20 feet forward and buckling the tracks into grotesque patterns. *The Engineer* of 20 December 1918 reported the event later: 'Cracks developed in the wall at various points. They caused a loud report, and as an air-raid was in progress at the time, the impression prevailed in the neighbourhood that bombs were being dropped by hostile aircraft in the vicinity'.

Trains were held up for two weeks and GCR services via Wycombe were diverted from Northolt Junction down the GWR into Paddington. The repair work involved reducing the gradient of the bank and strengthening the wall. But over the years since there has been minor trouble and reports of buildings cracking and subsiding gardens, so the tunnel was the correct way after all.

Wembley Hill station was provided with four tracks and a small goods yard, and it would appear from a picture of the station taken just before it opened that it had been intended to name it 'Wembley Park'. The double-track GCR Line crossed the LNWR line on a steel bridge that was designed for four lines, a flourish of optimism that was never fulfilled. At Sudbury, the booking office was at road level, with steps leading up to the wooden

London pride
A Great Central 4-4-0 locomotive, well polished and with steam up, acts as an improvised photographic platform. In the first years of the London Extension, these impressive locomotives were teamed with elegant coaching stock, including clerestory restaurant cars.

The last Joint Line timetable before nationalisation.

Unusual 'through' tickets on the Joint Line.

platforms. 'The goods yard is provided with goods warehouses and offices, horse and cattle dock, cattle pens and crane', confided a local paper, reporting on the opening of the line.

The next station was at Sudbury Hill, the pleasant road leading up to Harrow Hill. Opened as 'South Harrow', possibly to avoid confusion with the District Railway's Sudbury Hill station a few yards south, the name was confusing to residents and visitors. On 19 July 1926 the name was altered to Sudbury Hill (Harrow). With the opening of the GCR line, the station became a terminus for a short time of the first passenger services on the line (1 March to 2 April 1906). The service was worked by a revolutionary vehicle – a petrol-electric rail car powered by a 90hp engine. The rail car had a top speed of 40 mph and seated 50 passengers in four compartments.

Beyond 'South Harrow', the line passed through a 203-yard-long tunnel under the slopes of Harrow Hill and the District Railway. Provision was made at the western end of the tunnel for double tracks to connect with the District Railway, but the lines were never laid.

The railway then crossed the low lying marshy fields of Roxeth and Field End to join the GWR new line by means of a fly-under connection.

Northolt Junction had no station until 1908. Not that it was surprising, as all this part of Ruislip parish was then open fields. The Ruislip-Northwood Council petitioned for a station in January 1904 whilst work on the line was still in progress. Eventually the Joint Committee agreed and a station was opened in July 1908.

The then newly formed Ruislip-Northwood Urban District Council were one of the first local authorities in the country to produce a town plan under the Housing & Town Planning Act of 1909. The Council's ambitious project was for a Garden City, with 'Victoria Avenue' running from Northwood southwards to Northolt Junction. Incidentally, the 'Junction' was nowhere near Northolt Village and was eventually renamed South Ruislip. Between Northolt Junction and Ruislip and Ickenham provision was made for four tracks, the second pair coming into use a couple of years after the opening of the line. The station at Ruislip and Ickenham was sited midway between

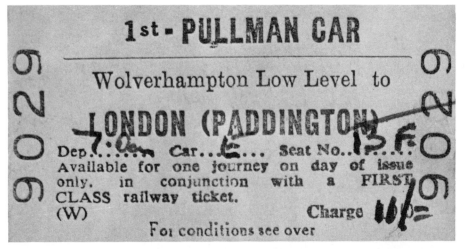

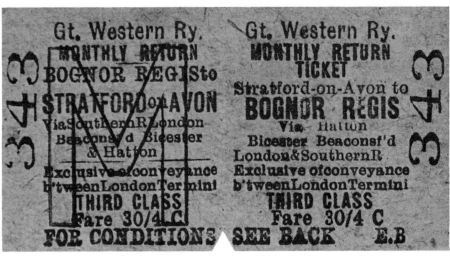

the two picturesque old villages and was built in red brick similar to Greenford.

The contractors' locomotives crossed the old road here on the level during the building work and there were delays to farm carts. In April 1903, a road steam engine hauling a massive trailer carrying the 30-ton girders for the road bridge shed its load in the Cowley Road at Uxbridge, holding up the odd farm cart, bicycles, and other sparse road traffic in that town for some hours. The new line continued across a corner of Ickenham Green (or common) and on through the open fields through Short Hill cutting to pass south of Harefield, and out across the Colne Valley into Buckinghamshire.

The bridges and the Grand Junction Canal Viaduct were built of best quality Staffordshire blue bricks. Just before the viaduct the 'Y' shaped junction for the line down the valley to Uxbridge was built. Work on this branch was not complete until 1907.

Much trouble was encountered with establishing a firm foundation in the marshy ground for the embankments at the junction. Thousands of tons of Welsh stone had to be laid down before

a firm foundation could be made. In order to keep the surrounding land dry, a pumping station was built in the angle of the 'Y' shape junction. The pump house supplied the water to the Ickenham pick up troughs on the line by Ickenham Green for many years.

During the building of the line at Denham, a serious accident occurred. In March 1902 one of the Manning-Wardle locomotives became derailed and its driver, Richard Pilkington, was killed. Local people got up a fund for his family and he was commemorated by a specially commissioned tombstone in Hillingdon Cemetery. Another accident near Denham involved the locomotive *Dunragit*, in January 1903, when a navvy seriously injured his hand when he caught it in a coupling whilst he was watching shunting. He had to be rushed by horse trap to Uxbridge Hospital, which by this time had become well used to dealing with injuries received by the men on the line.

Derailments were also frequent on the construction track. The locomotive *Gerrards Cross* came off the line at the temporary level crossing at Ruislip in 1903.

After Denham, the Chiltern Hills

Map of the Eastern's London suburban lines in 1947, when the Great Western and Great Central Joint Line was under LNER control. Marylebone is now under 'Midland' region.

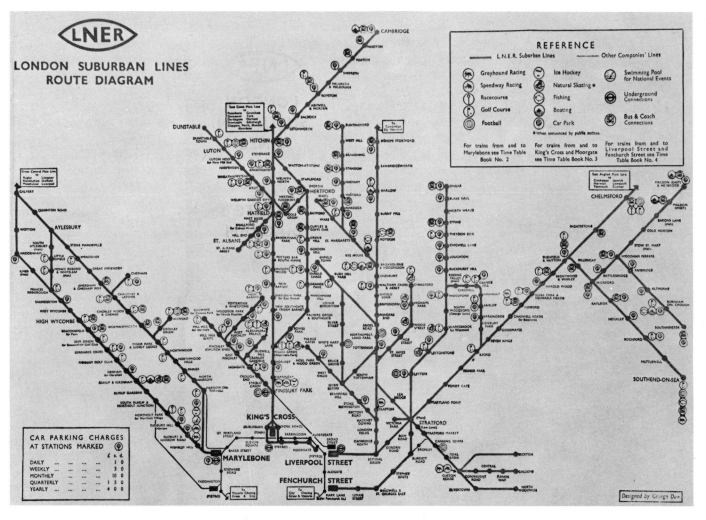

33

Early Edwardian 'Mini'
The country horse-and-trap was the runabout of the Edwardian age. Young ladies drove these light vehicles with confidence, perhaps collecting their parents from the London train.

were reached and the line was made through a series of deep cuttings. One of the deepest being at Gerrards Cross, where 1,228 cubic tons of chalk were excavated over a distance of 1½ miles at an average depth of 45 feet. More cuttings and short sections of embankment follow to Beaconsfield, where again there is a very deep cutting of 85 feet. Near Beaconsfield the line was cut through the beech woods of the Wilton Park estate, the home of the Du Pre family since 1780. Much of the material dug out here was used to fill in a deep dell in the woods near the present Baring Road, whilst other material remaining was used to make up the high embankments above. Loudwater on the approach to White House tunnel between Beaconsfield and High Wycombe. Between Gerrards Cross and Beaconsfield the highest point on the line above sea level is reached at 315 feet near Seer Green.

During the construction of the 348-yard-long White House tunnel six men lost their lives. After the tunnel the high embankment leads on to the 66-yard-long Penn Viaduct, also known as Sir Philip Rose's viaduct. He was a local landowner and he insisted that it was to be faced with red bricks instead of

Staffordshire blue so that it would blend with the surroundings.

The old Wycombe railway from Maidenhead came up the Wye valley from the south a short distance before High Wycombe. The original track was completely relaid and the cutting widened. Very extensive works were required at High Wycombe. There was insufficient room on the side of the steep hill above the town for four tracks and two facing platforms, so the 'up' platform was rebuilt south of the station, the far end of the 'down' platform having a subway connecting with the new 'up' platform. The existing station buildings on the 'down' side were completely rebuilt.

The whole job cost £18,000. It gave growing High Wycombe a station that was in keeping with its status as one of the principle towns in the Chilterns. A massive wall was rebuilt to hold back the hillside opposite the down platform – using 1¼ million of those Staffordshire blue bricks that were such a feature of the bridges on the line. The final cost for the building of the line from Northolt Junction to Wycombe was £11.50p per yard of double track, or £561,735 for the 23 miles. Further extensive works were required to widen

the route of the original single track line beyond High Wycombe.

One of the major works was the great cutting at Saunderton which was 2¼ miles long and included a tunnel. The original line then became the 'down' track. The new line was built on a gradient of 1/167 to the east of the original route in order to reduce the gradient for the high speed running of expresses, the original alignment having been too steep.

The High Wycombe-Princes Risborough-Haddenham section was built by Mackay and Davies of Cardiff, while L.P. Nott was the contractor for the 19½ miles from Haddenham to Ashendon Junction, and for the spur through Wotton to link the GCR's line to its original route at Grendon Underwood.

The divergence of the GCR and GWR lines at Ashendon was laid out with a fly-under as at Northolt Junction.

The GWR line through to Aynho via Bicester, known as the Bicester Cut-off, was begun in 1905. The route ran across the Vale of Aylesbury and through some rocky outcrops of the Cotswolds. It was surveyed by W.W. Grierson of the GWR, with Edward Perry and J.C. Inglis (who were also

responsible for High Wycombe station works) assisting. The contract was let to Scott and Middelton, with R.C. Sikes as the resident engineer. The work proceeded rapidly, including the construction of the 1147-yard-long Ardley Tunnel and the Ardley viaduct on the approach to the old GWR line from Oxford at Aynho Junction. In fact, the tunnel was completed in the short space of 18 months.

The ownership of the various sections of the new line were:

Old Oak Common to Northolt Junction	GWR
Neasden to Northolt Junction	GCR
Northolt Junction to Ashendon Junction	GWR/GCR
Denham-Uxbridge and Greenford-West Ealing	GWR
Princes Risborough-Aylesbury	GWR
Ashendon Junction to Grendon Underwood	GCR
Ashendon Junction to Aynho Junction	GWR
Aynho Junction-Birmingham-existing GWR line.	

From Aynho Junction the expresses would run over the existing GWR line through Banbury, Leamington Spa to Birmingham, opened in 1852.

Steam power on the land
Steam ploughing in the Chilterns about 1906. A major step towards farm mechanisation was the system of using steam power to draw a wheeled set of tines from one side of the field to the other by steel ropes which were drawn around a drum of a steam traction engine on the far side, the wire being released from a companion machine opposite. The operation needed skill and could only usefully be carried out on fields of generally regular shape. Labourers assisted the trained operators, one of whom is standing beside the steering column of the device. Steam power had been used in almost every capacity by the turn of the century.

The New Railway Opens

One Monday, 2 April 1906, all the men who had worked for some ten years to bring the railway into Marylebone and then out of London again to Princes Risborough and beyond, ceased their labours. For this was the day that the first trains ran, carrying special guests to celebrate the opening of the Great Western & Great Central Joint Railway in High Wycombe Town Hall. It was a large gathering, for officials of the two railways had to be accommodated. After the luncheon the trains that had brought the guests separately from Paddington and from Marylebone were joined, and the double-sized train puffed its way through the green desert of the Vale of Aylesbury and over the Great Central main line as far as Calvert, a station that the Great Central had created in the middle of nowhere and named after Sir Ralph Verney, a nearby landowner.

The line that opened that day had cost £40,000 a mile and the great question everybody asked was 'will the new line pay?'

It had been built to capture fast business traffic, but bad land slips in some of the steeper banks had already cost the company much money, so express trains were not able to run at once. One popular facility available to passengers was that their ticket was valid at either Paddington (via the Great Western) or at Marylebone.

And from a railwayman's point of view, High Wycombe stood poised for a great renaissance – newly linked direct with the north and west and, in a few more years when the Great Western Railway completed its link, with Birmingham as well. One of the speakers at the opening luncheon, indeed, was carried away with the great possibilities: 'The new line has put High Wycombe in direct communication with the bloaters of Yarmouth and the herrings of Lowestoft' he assured them.

Not everybody in the little Chilterns town joined in the general self-congratulations; many local gentlemen still moved uneasily around the town pressing heavily on their sticks, with grumbles upon their moustaches. To

Sentinel of an Imperial age
A London bobby, with Edwardian whiskers, is a still and silent witness to the Great Central's first triumph – its establishment as a London railway. The station booksellers at Marylebone display the sentimental sepia prints of the day, ready for framing in some of the new housing around London. Boards advertise desirable properties in Buckinghamshire, while a large railway placard boasts of its train services to England, Scotland and Ireland.

them, the railway was an invasion of vandals into the quietude they sought after an active business life. They had to be a little nifty upon their feet, though, because an even worse invasion was already well under way – the invasion of the Chiltern Hills by the motor car.

'Now one can visit Buckinghamshire places that have been so near yet so far', the speaker droned on. 'The new line has fine curves and goods yards with an eye on the future – a contrast to the old Maidenhead line which was cheap, and tainted with nastiness.' The organ at the Town Hall was played by S.M.A. Galpin, whilst the guests ate the ritually elaborate celebration lunch. The traders of Wycombe felt that the future prosperity and growth of the town were assured, but there were also those who were concerned that the new line should not spoil the beauty of the Chiltern Hills.

Two final sections of the new works remained to be opened. The line from Princes Risborough to Aynho ('The Bicester Cut-off') and the branch down

the Colne Valley to Uxbridge from Denham. The Press looked forward to the completion of the branch, which was planned to link up eventually (via the goods yard) with the original GWR station at Vine Street.

Construction costs of the Uxbridge branch were £87,459. The river Colne was crossed with a short steel bridge and the terminus was built on an embankment at the bottom of High Street, near the county boundary with Buckinghamshire. The embankment was built to enable the double-track line to be extended across the street and so round to Vine Street, and the girders of the bridge were actually laid across High Street. But despite endless promises the extension was never built. During the construction of the High Street terminus, a famous Uxbridge landmark disappeared – a 200-year-old plane tree – 17 feet in diameter and 70 feet high. It was felled by J. Lavender of Ruislip; the doomed plane, an early immigrant, toppling with a tremendous crash at 12.30 pm on 13 July 1906. The passenger service from Gerrards Cross opened on 24 April 1907, but

Starting the special train
On 9 March 1899, the Rt Hon. C.T. Richie, MP, President of the Board of Trade, on Platform 2 at the new Marylebone terminus of the GCR pulled a silver lever connected to the locomotive 861. It puffed slowly away, marking the Official opening of the station. It was held beyond the bridge, amid a chorus of whistles from its sister locomotives, and was later brought back to the station to haul the 4.28 pm special to Rugby and Manchester. Passenger services began on Wednesday, 15 March 1899.

goods trains did not get going until 11 May 1914.

The final opening – from Aynho, south of Banbury to Bicester and Risborough took place on 4 April 1910, when goods trains began running from Aynho to Risborough. The passenger train service began on Friday 1 July 1910 running to Paddington via the new route.

Press and publicity broke out into renewed heights of exaltation:

'The new GWR line opens up a region of phenomenal beauty which has somehow or other managed to retain, notwithstanding its proximity to London most of the old world charms which have vanished from more remote areas.'

'The new line will open up rural Bucks . . . a land asleep since the days of the stage coach.'

'The new line traverses 23 miles of verdant tranquility.'

It seemed too good to be true.

Over fifty years of busy activity had begun.

Marylebone: early days

With the completion of the lines, the Great Central, perhaps more than the GWR, saw the potential of developing what we would now call commuter traffic. Trains made up of 5-coach sets of carriages in varnished teak were built for the Marylebone suburban services in 1911. The carriages were by far the most luxurious any London commuter line had yet seen. In the first class compartments there were shoulder-height reading lamps, and foot stools on which tired businessmen could rest their feet and relax with the *Evening News* or *Star* on the home journey to their new half-timbered or Queen Anne style villas amid the beeches. They could feel safe in the knowledge that one of Mr Robinson's 4-6-2 tank engines would get them there in time for their pre-dinner sherry.

The GCR was anxious to develop its commuter traffic as it looked over its shoulder at the success of the Metropolitan's publicity (and what we now call marketing) which was about to

The new terminus

The Great Central's new Marylebone terminus. Coal trains began using the new line on 25 July 1898 and eight months later, when the track had bedded down, the first passenger train left the station. 'The results of the early traffic are regarded as eminently satisfactory', said the *Railway Magazine*.

Coaling in the fifties
An ex-Great Central Robinson tank locomotive coaling outside Marylebone station in the 1950s. This 4-4-2 tank, at this time running as No. 69805, was one of a breed of very stately locomotives.

develop its theme of 'Metro-land'. So the publicity people at Marylebone got their heads together, and in tune with the general movement towards garden cities and the open air life, devised the slogan:

'The Great Central Railway is the Line of Health'.

Publications such as T.W.D. Smith's *Strolls in Beechy Bucks*, promoted the Chilterns as an adventure playground for Londoners, although the GWR also encouraged people to live there with its *Homes For All in London's Western Borderland*, which was published quarterly until July 1914. There was a similar GWR publication for the other end of the line, advertising new homes in the outskirts of Birmingham, published from January 1912. In order to provide better connections to the centre of London, the Bakerloo Tube was extended from Baker Street to Marylebone on 27 March 1907, the Tube station at Marylebone being called Great Central, which seems to have been a publicity triumph of Sir Sam Fay's. The name was changed to Marylebone on 12 May 1917. Yet despite the introduction of new commuter services and the additional expresses via the High Wycombe line, the dream of making Marylebone a great and busy terminus like Paddington or St Pancras was ever to elude the GCR. Between rush hours and at weekends it was the only London terminus, according to one writer: 'where you could hear birdsong'.

'The GCR at Marylebone Station . . . quietest and most dignified of all stations, where the porters go on tiptoe, where barrows are rubber tyred and the trains rattle mysteriously in and out with only the faintest of toots upon their whistles so as not to distract the signalman!'

A.G. O'Donnell, in his *England, their England* has, perhaps, the most evocative description of all. With a little licence, it could still apply to the diesel era today at Marylebone! 'The station was silent. The newspaper boy was asleep. A horse, waiting all harnessed to a loaded van, yawned. The dust filtered slowly down through the winter sunbeams, gradually obliterating a label upon a wooden crate which read "Urgent, perishable".'

Marylebone was essentially the terminus of the wealthy commuters of Gerrards Cross and Beaconsfield, and country folk up to town from the Vale of Aylesbury. It briefly sprang to life only at other times when an express arrived from Manchester or Sheffield. But even then the trains were not regularly filled.

The Train Services

For a great many years the pattern of services was fairly consistent. The GWR ran most of the express trains, the LNER expresses, successors to those magnificent Great Central trains, being less in evidence (as many ran via the Harrow and Aylesbury (Met) route).

London suburban traffic, however, was mainly in the hands of the LNER, whilst the GWR used its auto-trains with their saloon carriages and 0-6-0 tank engines – popularly known as the 'push and pulls'. These trains ran out from Paddington or Ealing and called at the various halts and stations up to Ruislip. The outer GWR stopping trains worked through to Aylesbury or Oxford. There was a pattern of stopping trains (once again of the 'push and pull' type) starting from Princes Risborough.

In GCR days, the Marylebone suburban trains were initially worked with 9K and 9L 4-4-2 tank engines, but after 1911 the 'Coronation' tanks (9N class) took over. The GCR carriages were fitted with huge fenders or 'over-riders' to lessen the danger of telescoping in case of accident. But one wonders why more attention wasn't paid to the possible cause of collisons! However, we are being less than fair, for apart from a collision outside Marylebone on 28 March 1913, there was little trouble over the years.

In 1916, the GCR installed the Relio-stop Mechanical Brake Control System between Marylebone and Wembley Hill, extending to Northolt Junction in 1919. In 1922/23 one of the first daylight colour light signal systems was installed in connection with the building of the Exhibition Loop Line at Wembley and came into use on 8 April 1923.

By the 1930s the carriages were of the LNER 'teak' type, usually in articulated sets, stock which lasted until the end of the 1950s when they were replaced for a short time by LMS

Paddington

This old view was taken about 1910. Posters advertise 'GWR, new route: London, Leamington Spa 1 hr 31 mins. Stratford-on-Avon 2 hrs 10 mins.' It must be summer, as the young men are wearing their straw boaters. The train has a clerestory slip-coach. You can just see the vacuum brake reservoir tanks along its roof.

In this orderly Edwardian world, a young man and young lady wait patiently for the arrival of country friends, and an old gentleman hurries with a large 'Oscar Wilde' type hand-bag.

Marylebone
Ready to go! This 4-6-2 tank locomotive manages to keep its dignified lines in spite of the apparent neglect of its paintwork in British Railways days. The scene at Marylebone shows the afternoon departure for Woodford Halse in July 1954.

compartment stock until the introduction of diesel multiple unit trains in 1961.

Perhaps one of the most interesting features about the GWR services was the practice of including slip coaches on express trains. These were carriages fitted with front windows and specially controlled apparatus, worked by a 'slip' guard. It was his job to release the couplings by means of the apparatus from the main train, and bring the slip coach gently to a stop at one of the scheduled stations, whilst the main train could run non-stop between say Paddington and Birmingham. The 4.00 pm from London at one time dropped coaches at Bicester, Leamington Spa and Knowle, whilst the 6.05 pm from London did the same from Banbury, Leamington and Lapworth. At one time a slip coach was dropped even for Gerrards Cross, where a waiting locomotive took it on to Beaconsfield and High Wycombe.

The LNER also had trains with slip coaches. For some years the Marylebone to Bradford, via High Wycombe, expresses would slip two coaches beyond Grendon Underwood, where a waiting engine would take it on to Woodford Halse.

But it was the GWR who perpetuated the practice into British Railways days. The very last service to

be worked with slip coaches was on the Joint line. The 5.10 pm from Paddington was the last train in Britain to 'slip'. This historic event took place at Bicester on 9 September 1960 at 6.12 pm. The Bicester slip would be dropped short of Bicester platform and drawn into the station by the engine of a slow train, which then proceeded to Banbury. It was the extra staff required, as well as great acceleration of modern diesel locomotives which finally put an end to this interesting practice.

Barry Morgan in his book *The Compleat Imbiber* (1956) recalls the delights on travel on the 5.10 from Paddington: ' . . . such as the hour when you get up from tea . . . and watch them drop the Bicester slip coach, and then settle down to the first evening drink.'

In the early years of the new line, GWR expresses were usually in charge of 'Star' class locomotives. But the increasing traffic between London and the Midlands and heavier, faster trains, saw them superseded by the 'Castles' and 'Kings'. There were also some odd workings. Incredible as it would seem to us today, there was once a GWR steam rail motor service (1905/15) from Joint line stations to Victoria! The route was via Greenford, North Acton, then over the Wood Lane line to Kensington and Clapham Junction.

The opening up of the GWR line made the LNER make even more efforts to attract passengers to its Euston-Birmingham service. A through train, with typing and secretarial facilities, was announced from Birmingham (New Street) to London (Broad Street). The GWR replied with a through express from Birmingham (Snow Hill) to London (Victoria).

During the 20s and 30s, the GWR route was popular because of its attractive scenery. With growing numbers of tourists – especially from the United States, the *Shakespeare Express* was put on at 9.25 am from Paddington to Stratford-upon-Avon, via Leamington Spa. In 1931 special luggage labels were supplied for this train reading: 'Passenger by London (Paddington) to Stratford-on-Avon *Shakespeare Express*'.

Edward J. Burroughs Limited published in 1925 for the GWR a series of route guides, one being 'Through the window . . . Paddington to Birkenhead'. The Colne Valley, the beechy Chalfonts, the hill at West Wycombe with the Dashwood Mausoleum and church tower with its golden ball on top, were all features for the traveller to look for as his train sped along.

Another named train was *The Cambrian Coast Express* which ran on Fridays and Saturdays in the summer, leaving Paddington at 10.10 am. Yet another GWR-named express was the 4.10 pm from Paddington, which ran through to Birkenhead. It was known as *The Belfast Boat Express*. In connection with the rivalry previously mentioned with the LNWR (LMS), the GWR for some years advertised its expresses with a series of posters with the slogan: '2 hours shortest route' and a businessman in bowler hat and white spats shaking the smug driver's hand and saying: 'Splendid run! Thank you!' (The two-hour expresses left London at 9.10 am, 11.10 am, 2.10 pm, 4.10 pm, 6.10 pm and 7.10 pm). 'As the crow flies', another poster, boasted a map of the route.

During the inter-war years goods traffic was not heavy by the standards of the other main lines from London to the North and West, but bearing in mind the rural aspects of much of the new line's route, 25 goods trains a day each way was a fairly good tonnage.

The greatest change on the line came in the late 1930s, with work arising from the extension of London Transport's Central Line from North Acton to Ruislip (and the proposed projection on to Denham) as part of the London Transport New Works programme of 1935/40. The new line was built parallel to the old line and

Marylebone
A somewhat different location for a locomotive one normally associates with King's Cross. No. 60103 'Flying Scotsman' is seen here at rest with 'The South Yorkshireman' express on 7 July 1952. This popular train was introduced on 31 May 1948 and ran via the Joint Line and Ashendon Junction to Bradford.

new stations were to replace the existing GWR halts and stations. The work began with modernisation of the existing parts of the Central Line from Wood Lane (later replaced by White City) to Acton before the Second World War. This was the original Ealing and Shepherd's Bush Railway opened by GWR for goods in 1917 and electrified for Central Line trains in 1920. The GWR was responsible for the new work. Out at Ruislip Gardens rebuilding of the bridge over West End Road had to be carried out without disruption of rail traffic. The Second World War was well into its first year before work was completed because of unforeseen trouble with water under the GWR embankments. Incredibly, some of the girders were swung into place at night during the black-out, with the use of arc-lamps! When the GWR wanted a job done properly it *was*, Hitler notwithstanding!

One of the major works apart from the new stations, was a fly-under junction and sections of concrete viaduct at Greenford for the Ealing GWR trains to come into Greenford

new station without having to cross the Central Line tracks. There was also the widening of the deep cutting beyond Northolt. By far the greatest work was the laying out of the extensive train depot between Ruislip Gardens and West Ruislip. It was said to be one of the first major civil engineering projects in Britain to use bulldozers.

With some of the tracks laid down the stations well under way, the War began to drain the labour force and supplies. The new track at Greenford and places south was 'borrowed' for standby use elsewhere on the Underground and all work eventually came to a complete halt.

Troop trains, munition trains, disrupted services, lack of lighting at night, the building of additional sidings and depots were all part of the War scene. Even remote halts like Ilmer, Dorton, Haddenham, and Ardley, as well as Blackthorn, became busy with RAF and Army personnel. At one time the LNER Timing Office was housed in a concrete bunker-type building at Gerrards Cross. But after the war, work on the Central Line was resumed

Outward bound
The Wolverhampton express begins its journey with *King William III* in charge. Built in 1928, she was withdrawn in 1962.

and the first trains reached Greenford on 30 June 1947, the old GWR halts being closed from that date. Greenford was unique at that time in being the only London Transport station with an escalator that took passengers up to the trains on the viaduct above.

The extension out to West Ruislip followed. The Official opening train ran on Friday, 19 November 1948 – passenger services beginning on 21 November 1948 when the GWR local service was withdrawn. Only the Greenford-Ealing shuttle then remained. The pattern of suburban trains was then worked from Marylebone to High Wycombe or Princes Risborough, with stopping trains operated by Western Region from Princes Risborough to Bicester and Banbury and the Watlington – Thame lines.

The express trains continued to carry a large number of passengers. *The Cambrian Coast Express* became a daily train. The train ran beyond Birmingham to Wolverhampton, Shrewsbury, Barmouth, Pwllheli and Aberystwyth. There was also the

'Inter-City' Express (long before this became the general term for express trains!) and a brochure was issued telling passengers the various interesting features they could see on the route. This train left Paddington at 8.20 am with the first stop at High Wycombe.

For a time the old order of things prevailed as Western Region express rolling stock reverted to GWR-style brown and cream livery, with locomotives in GWR green. The trains made a splendid sight as they hurried on a sunny morning through the deep Chilterns at West Wycombe or along the 'racing ground' from Ashenden to Bicester, creating memories of the 1930s. The principal express from Marylebone was *The Master Cutler*. But after 1958, the *Cutler* was switched to St Pancras and the Midland Line to Sheffield. After that date the number of LNER expresses using the Joint Line declined.

The Marylebone management was passed from Eastern Region to the Western for a time and it was possible on occasions to travel in GWR compartment stock and even corridor sets on a High Wycombe stopping train starting from Marylebone! The line is now under the Midland Region.

Perhaps the next exciting event on the line in the early 1960s was the introduction of the 'Blue Pullman' diesel multiple-unit trains, which ran from Paddington to Wolverhampton. Painted in an attractive blue and white, they were the forerunners of today's '125' sets. But trying to balance a hot cup of coffee whilst sitting at the table in either the front or rear cars as the trains raced through Ruislip or Haddenham was a challenge calling for great balancing skill, and a large newspaper to mop up spillage!

From January 1961, the roar of diesel multiple-unit trains began to be heard at Marylebone and the last steam suburban train to leave was in June 1962. Western Region cross country diesel units were also used on some of the GWR services. The 'Castles' and 'Kings' gave way to the maroon-coloured 'Westerns'. Traffic remained busy during the years when the Euston line was being electrified in the 1960s until Dr Beeching's writing became ever clearer on the wall. It was to end with the closure of Snow Hill, that great cathedral of the railway age in Birmingham, in 1967.

Envoi

After 1958, Marylebone trains only used the Ashenden Junction–Grendon Underwood line about twice a week and it finally closed on 3 September 1967, although the last trains had officially run over this route in September 1966.

The very last regular express train arrived in Marylebone station at 5.23 am on 4 September 1966. From that day Marylebone ceased to be a main line terminus. *The Cambrian Coast Express* roared through the Chilterns for the last time on Saturday 4 March 1967. At Princes Risborough, the local and branch services were closed. The last passenger trains ran on the Watlington branch on 29 June 1957. On the Bourne End to High Wycombe section of the original Wycombe Railway the last train ran on 4 May 1969. Even the useful connection from Princes Risborough to Thame and Oxford, which for so long had seen relief trains and all kinds of traffic, was closed to passengers on 7 January 1963. At the same time the smaller stations and halts on the main line closed, leaving only Bicester open.

However, the single track line up to Aylesbury remains today – although with trains only at peak hours. Freight trains still run down the Watlington branch as far as Chinnor Cement works under the Chiltern ridges, and to Thame oil depot.

By 1981 there was one express train working from Birmingham (New Street) to Paddington via High Wycombe. The train still stops at Princes Risborough (now only the 'Up' platform is in use) at 8.22 am and the station becomes very busy with commuters who use this popular train for a quick run to London. In the evening the return from Paddington is at 5.42 pm and tube train travellers at Greenford or West Ruislip are often surprised to see the train roar through, with the buffet car doing a busy trade! There is a regular service of trains from Marylebone to Banbury, where the frequent expresses from Didcot and Oxford can be joined for the onward journey to Birmingham (New Street) via Leamington and Coventry.

And the future? There have been moves over the years to close Marylebone and run the Wycombe trains to Paddington. The number of freight trains have dwindled; goods yards have been closed and even the once popular weekend special trains in the summer are less in number than they were in the 1970s. The trains are lightly loaded beyond Princes Risborough and if services were reinstated between the old LMS at Bicester and Oxford, the passenger line to Banbury could be closed. So after a life of only 70 or so years, the last steam line built in England has fallen on hard times and faces a bleak future.

The Railway's Influence on Social Change

Although the new railway did not appear to affect all little rural communities of the Vale of Aylesbury, the lives of those who spent their lives on the land were quickly altering in subtle ways. Farm labourers as a class formed a large part of the rural population – the 'poor man at the gate' of the large estates that still dictated the whole regime of the countryside's year.

Between 1850, at the start of the great Railway Age, and the start of the First World War, despite increases in farm mechanisation, this solid peasantry had declined by only one-third.

Yet the railways, right from their early days, had a strong influence on these men. For a start, many of these people were taken on (as a temporary basis) to swell the number of 'professional' navvies who had been in almost continuous employment

Saunderton
A 'Castle' with a London train passes through Saunderton cutting.

Paddington
Typical evening scene in the 1950s, with *Stokesey Castle* taking a rest after arriving with an express from Birmingham. Built in 1935, she was withdrawn in 1963.

constructing the Great Central Railway's extension into London at the turn of the century, and out again, a decade later, to the Chilterns at High Wycombe. Some of these locals found themselves plate-laying; others filled in as waggoners.

And although things had moved off the poverty line for these farm labourers as the railways allowed the flow of cheap grain and other basic substances, this more regular and reliable employment with a major industry did to some degree stablize the decline that had become evident in the villages of Buckinghamshire and Oxfordshire for some decades.

Of course, the new railway also encouraged the drift into London. Most country families knew at least one relative who had gone into London to seek a living. But once again, it was the coming of the railway, anxious to secure its revenue from every trivial little community along its path, that helped to break up some of the static nature of country life in this part of the Chilterns, and conveyed regular mail between town and country, so that people, although they were altering their way of life, kept in close contact.

Of course, around High Wycombe, the railway was no new toy, as we have seen, for the Great Western's line already linked the town with Maidenhead and with Princes Risborough. But we can imagine the

excitement that occurred in villages such as Haddenham and the hamlets such as Ilmer, when the huge earth embankments moved remorselessly towards them and their little world.

'When the railway first came, everyone in the street would hurry to the bridge so that they could see the smoke coming, and then watch the train rush underneath', remembered one old man from a farm near Haddenham. There was a feeling that here was something very new and terrible that made the bridges shake as they stood upon them, and which brought to all their lives the feeling of being in a larger and more wonderful world.

Small towns like Princes Risborough (to become a multiple railway junction with the arrival of the Joint line) and Bicester, quickly had railway jobs to offer local men, who had previously had little option but to work on the land, as their fathers had. Suddenly, in a blaze of uniforms, they appeared again as local station staff, or elsewhere on the railway system, bringing regular, if limited, wages into the village economy, and a sense of pride and self-respect to the men themselves. In the first decade of the 20th century in one village near Bicester, seven grooms, out of 39 couples married over a period, had employment as railwaymen. During this change, as the new line reached completion, village life kept this sense of evolution.

The Rural Poor and the Railway

There were few interests for local men, who worked long hours on the land in all weathers and on all days of the week, especially if there were animals to feed. There had been an attempt by a well-intended gentry to provide allotments in the early 1830s, so that honest 'John Bull' could provide fresh vegetables for his family, but the good people failed to grasp the fact that few men had the spare time to plod away on such a busman's holiday every week, and the local pubs kept their fascinating lure.

The Edwardian period, at the time the Joint Line was opened, was the climax of a social unease about poverty in England; a time when Seebohm Rowntree's investigation for his book *Poverty – a Study* (1901) suggested that one-third of England's population was on the edge of starvation. The situation was more obvious in the towns, but just as hard in the country areas where most could never spend a penny on a railway fare, 'purchase a half-penny newspaper or write a letter to absent children, for they cannot afford the postage'.

For village people, the church, and the chapel had given them a concern for the law and a pride, in spite of their lot, in being British, for the South African War veterans had returned to every parish, and already arising for anyone to see upon the highest promontory of the Chiltern Hills, was a memorial to the Fallen.

In another of Rowntree's books, *How the Labourer Lives* (1913), a labourer, Mr West, said that his regular wage was twelve shillings, which he could lose in wet weather. His wife said 'whatever happens, you will never hear a word from him in the way of grumbling – he's a Christian man. He just takes things as they come'.

To such people a new railway, as any sign of change, was regarded as an

Countrywomen from North Oxfordshire
A peasant woman and her daughter. Nobody was dressed in those days without the inevitable shawl. The elder woman's face is lined with a sort of resigned humour – witness to the hard life in rural England in the early years of this century. A train trip into nearby Banbury would have been a once-yearly luxury for such a woman, and she would busy herself with straw-plaiting or her needle, for time meant money to the poor.

49

opportunity for employment, yet as a possible threat to their precarious way of life. Little was available to fill the family pot in the way of extras, apart from a rabbit or two, or a brace of birds from the local landowner as a Christmas perk for the family. One of the Engineering contractors on the Joint Line through the Chilterns remembered the countryman, even when recruited as a railway worker, never forgot his skill at foraging: 'My ganger, Bill Langston, was an inveterate poacher. Every time he could, he would go out into the Buckinghamshire countryside and pit his wits against the local game-keepers. He never came back empty-handed, and I never heard of him being summoned for "trespassing in pursuit of conies".'

Railway workers on the new Joint Line had the same need for 'potboys' as their brothers had on the land. Gallons of potent local brew maintained the old fears about wife-bashing and family privation that had long been emotive rallying points for the anti-drink campaign puritans – a cause that had been going on for the previous fifty years.

It was customary during the building of the railway for a colony of navvies' huts to be placed near a major job – such as the deep cutting at Gerrards Cross. As they were frequently sited miles from the nearest village pub, usually barrels of beer were kept on the site for the men, so that they could have it with their breakfast. It was purchased wholesale at about one shilling a gallon, and had plenty of '6X – Extract of malt and hops' about it. Nearer the villages, the railway construction teams would set off to taste the company of the local pub, with sometimes lusty and unpleasant results. Occasionally the noise from a travelling band of players would be heard in the villages, making the dogs bark and the children dance, and providing a little village gossip. Most families provided their own music, gathered around the inevitable piano, singing songs that have long been forgotten.

Farm mechanisation had arrived

with tedious slowness; the great milestones were, perhaps, the steam plough and the various marks of reaper-binders. Yet these new machines could be lethal in the hands of men used to the lazy sweep of the scythe. One early 'rack' machine (which had revolving sails which brought the corn to the blade and also passed it free from the machine) gave rise to many accidents to men who were unused to thinking and working with anything other than hand tools. Farm working had always been extremely dangerous – falls from stacks and moving waggons were common.

It is easy to see why the railway, with its careful training, the use of power, and the *esprit de cours* could very easily seem to be a gift from the Divine Providence; worthy to be praised in the local village chapel (another ubiquitous institution that, like the railway, could be found in almost every hamlet of Edwardian England).

We have introduced into this book illustrations showing the early competition to the Great Western & Great Central Joint Line from road transport, which was, in the end, to prove dominant. One lady at Beaconsfield said, after witnessing a motor-car accident in 1908: 'It is all very well having these monsters confined to iron rails, but once let loose upon the road, it is complete disaster.'

However, the competition was, at first, insignificant. People travelled in to the stations on the new line by horse and cart and it was only gradually that the old horse bus and carriers' waggons were replaced by the motor bus. There was little early attempt at carrying goods by road for any distance except by steam-fired waggons, because it was uneconomical and unreliable to transport by road. Of course, as the motor age swept into its full power after the First World War, so the railway carriage of goods stabilised and then slowly declined.

It was the beginning of the end – the Great Western & Great Central Joint Line had been built in the wrong countryside and several decades too late . . .

Opposite

To Norway by way of Sudbury!
With today's rationalisation of railway routes, the railways have lost most of their interesting trains. It is difficult to imagine going to Immingham and boarding a liner for a cruise around the rocky coasts of Norway, and travelling through the western suburbs of London and the Chilterns to get there! The boat trains ran on Fridays only in the summer months before the Second World War. This ex-GCR 'Lord Faringdon' class locomotive hurries through Sudbury and Harrow Road station with its wooden platforms with a Norway Cruise Boat Train in 1937.

Wonderful Wembley

FORWARD.

Wembley Hill

The building of the Great Central was carried out with mechanical as well as hand tools. This scene is near the site of the future Wembley Hill station and the contractors, Thomas Oliver and Sons have a useful, if rather Heath Robinson looking piece of equipment to help dig out the heavy London clay. On the hill above is the steel structure of 'Watkin's Folly'.

The first houses of what was to be Mostyn Avenue, Wembley Hill, can be seen, whilst in the middle distance is the lodge to the Park, known as Wembley Hill Cottage, the home of Harry William Smith.

The digging of the deep cutting here meant the removal of 640,000 cubic yards of spoil.

Wonderful Wembley

London at the time when the line was opened, extended only as far as Willesden, although there were small islands of houses at Neasden, and along the Harrow Road at Wembley. It was the British Empire exhibition at Wembley in 1924/5 that was to provide the stimulus to suburban development both along the Metropolitan Railway and the GCR through Wembley Hill and Sudbury.

The LNWR had had a station at Wembley since 1842 (called 'Sudbury') because Wembley itself was a mere hamlet. Wembley Hill rises 234 feet above the clay plain of Middlesex and is the first hill of any note on the line after it branches from the Met and GCR at Neasden. In the early 19th century the hill became a popular place to walk out to from London and the 'Green Man' at the top did a lively trade in refreshments. In 1837 it was described as 'A favourite Sunday resort

for a respectable class of person. The grounds which are perfectly laid out, command a very extensive panoramic view of the surrounding countryside, including the Metropolis'.

Wembley Park, sometimes known as the White House estate, extended over much of the hill and down to the pretty banks of the river Brent towards rural Neasden. In 1889 the executors of the last owner, John Gray, sold the estate to the Metropolitan Railway. It was the Metropolitan's dynamic Chairman, Sir Edward Watkin, (also Chairman of the GCR) who, following a visit to Paris, decided that London needed a tower to rival that of M. Eiffel. Wembley Park was chosen as the site of Watkin's Tower – mentioned briefly earlier. A competition to decide the best design of the Tower was held. From the mass of bizarre and amusing designs submitted the final choice was made of a tower very much like the Paris model. The Tower Company was formed in

October 1889 and 124 acres of Wembley Park leased to it for £2,000 pa for 999 years. The design was won by A.D. Stewart, J.M. MacLaren and W. Dunn with a 1200-foot-high tower, which was some 165 feet lower than Paris. The contract went to Heenan Froude in August 1891. The International Tower Construction Co. was reformed as the Metropolitan Tower Construction Company in October of that year. The great landmark was not only to provide a viewing platform for London, but would include restaurants, a theatre, dancing rooms, Turkish baths and 'rooms for exhibiting all kinds of scientific and amusing novelties'.

The engineer was the distinguished Sir Benjamin Baker of Forth Bridge fame. The first stage of the tower was completed in October 1895, although the pleasure grounds had already been opened from May 1894. The first stage of the tower was opened in May 1896 and the crowds were at last able to view the grassy slopes of distant Dollis Hill or the chimneys of the houses over at Willesden! In June 1897 the tower was illuminated and during the next few years a number of events were held in the grounds, including a test cricket match, as well as circuses.

But gradually the crowds dwindled. Wembley was still a journey into the unknown country and the tower did not look like getting any higher than the

150 feet of the first stage. In fact, the company ran out of money, the investors of enthusiasm, and by the time the GCR was being cut through the hillside near the Tower, there was already talk of the structure being demolished. Demolition by the same firm who built it began in 1907 and a special explosive called 'Roborite' was used to destroy the huge girders and part of the concrete bases. Some 2,700 tons of steel were salvaged and sent to Italy. Part of the grounds were sold for building, Oakington Avenue being one of the roads with 'high class residences with tennis courts and motor houses'. The rest remained virtually disused until the advent of the British Empire Exhibition after the First World War.

From Whit Monday 1909, the Tower grounds re-opened: 'It is hoped to turn it into a summer resort, combining the attractions of Earl's Court and the White City with rural country'. Both the Metropolitan and the Great Central hoped to build up pleasure traffic.

Even before the Great Central was built developers had been planning roads to Wembley Hill, and Walter Hill and Sons began estates in Dagmar Avenue, Mostyn Avenue and Dennis Avenue, although the later plans to extend Dennis Avenue had to be curtailed because the GCR line ran through the land.

These Edwardian years saw the

Wembley Hill station
This picture of 1904 shows Wembley Hill station after it had been open for only a short time. In the background are the slopes of Wembley Park. The signal box that can be seen on the right carried the name 'Wembley Park' during the construction of the station, but it appears that the GCR directors realised the confusion that would be caused with the Metropolitan's station of that name to the north of the park, and so changed the name to 'Wembley Hill'.

popularity of the Garden City and with the opening of the GCR and the GWR, the local papers saw the potential of building up traffic. 'We have several magnificent opportunities for these new towns and villages in our area – especially around the stations of the GCR at Ruislip and Ickenham, and the Seer Green and Jordan's area', said the *Middlesex Advertiser*. The Wembley Hill Garden Estate was the project of Sir Audley Dallas Neeld. He laid out two main 80-foot-wide roads on land south of Wembley Hill Station and when the official opening of the estate took place on 20 June 1914, there were 20 houses ready for occupation. The builders were Callow and Wright. None other than the garden city pioneer Ebenezer Howard was present at the opening ceremony. The plans were drawn up by R. Cracknell, and Marylebone was advertised as only '11 minutes away'.

Cup Final Day
The scene at Wembley Stadium Station on F.A. Cup Final Day, 24 April 1948. The station was visited by special trains hauled by rare locomotive visitors. Mr R. Wright, writing in *Journal of the Stephenson Locomotive Society* noted that he recorded the Great Eastern's 4-6-0s, Great Central and North Eastern Railway locomotives on duty during the twenties.

Hero of the hour
Half London made its way to see the First Cup Final at Wembley in 1923. It wasn't just the teams, but the attraction of the huge new concrete stadium, the first tangible evidence that the British Empire Exhibition would soon be a reality. The stadium was built for 100,000 people. By lunch time on that memorable Saturday, 23 April, 126,047 people had clicked through the turnstiles and the arithmetic went all wrong. Another 75,000 got in without paying, whilst outside thousands more arrived every minute!

The crowds began to move out on to the pitch. It was PC George Storey on 'Billie' who gently shunted them back to the edge. Disaster was averted and the constable has become a legend. At the top right-hand corner of the picture an LNER local is steaming along to Wembley Hill station, whilst at the top left of the picture, the ground is being prepared for the buildings of the Exhibition.

Wembley Park, the world comes to Wembley

'It will be a city of peep-shows and playhouses, cafes and restaurants, massed bands and movies – every class will be catered for, every taste, every desire for novelty, and the latest thrill, for the world has been ransacked for its side shows.' So the *Sunday Times* wrote about the British Empire Exhibition at Wembley.

Conceived as an idea by Lord Strathcona before the First World War, the great exhibition rose on the grasslands of Wembley Park where the Tower had stood and golf had been played. It became the largest concrete city in the world. Yet despite its popularity and its ideals celebrating the British Empire and its achievements, it was really a final show of the Empire before the sun began to go down. Its sprawl of buildings were old-fashioned-looking. It was a glorious celebration of the past. 'I declare the British Empire Exhibition open and pray by the blessing of God that it may conduce the unity and prosperity of my people and the peace and well-being of the world.' rang the guttural sounds of King George V's opening address on St George's Day 1924. It was the first time the monarch had spoken on the BBC. The Exhibition was a success and was repeated, perhaps less profitably, in 1925. Thousands came to Wembley for the first time and many came again and again to see the Exhibition and to explore the beauties of the local countryside.

Sudbury and Harrow Road
This picture must date from after 1910, because the tracks of the Metropolitan Electric Tramways can be seen. The trams reached the village of Sudbury after Wembley. Before the GCR line opened, passengers for London had to take the horse bus that ran from Harrow-on-the-Hill via 'The Swan', Sudbury, to the LNWR at Wembley High Road.

Northolt Park
Racing at Northolt Park course was a popular day's outing for many people in the 1930s. Laid out at Dabb's Hill, south of the GCR on the way to Northolt Junction, the course had a 1½-mile track, spectator stands, and all kinds of up-to-date race track facilities, including an electric totalisator and a course watering system. In 1938 the BBC brought along its TV cameras – one of the first outside sports broadcasts on the then very new medium. The LNER opened Northolt Park halt just by the bridge over the Roxeth-Northolt Road. The Second World War ended the races and the place became a military camp. When peace came there was just one night of final glory – Victory fireworks. Then after a few sad years of decay, the vast area was built over with council houses.

It was Lord Strathcona who first conceived the idea of 'An Imperial Industries Exhibition' in 1913. After the First World War the Government revived the idea. In 1920 an Act of Parliament empowered the government to guarantee £100,000, provided that a further amount of £50,000 was raised towards setting up the exhibition. The Metropolitan Railway put up £80,000 when Wembley Park, 'one of the most beautiful parks in London', was chosen as the venue. The exhibition was laid out on 216 acres and the first spade of earth was turned by the Duke of York at 3 pm on 11 January 1922. The main feature was the stadium, designed by Sir Owen Williams and Sir John Simpson. The builders were Sir Robert McAlpine, who employed 2,000 men – mainly ex-army, on the huge concrete structure which was sited on the high land above the GCR line at Wembley Hill. The stadium cost £750,000 and opened for the Cup Final on 23 April 1923. The exhibition opened on 23

April 1924. 'Let us go to Wembley where may be seen such wonders as have never before been gathered together in one place of the world', said the stirring words in the official catalogue.

'Wembley, itself a small world, stands before the world as an example of the courage and progress of the race'.

Next to the GCR station what was claimed as the world's first bus station was laid out. It covered 2 acres and could handle 20,000 people an hour, with General buses leaving every 15 seconds at peak times. In order to relieve pressure on Wembley Hill station, the GCR (by then the LNER) built a loop line at the eastern side of the exhibition grounds, with a single platform station in concrete. This line was designed to handle 16,000 passengers an hour and trains every 3 minutes were advertised. What was then the first main line application of daylight 3-aspect colour signals was installed and the Stadium Station

opened on 23 April 1923.

Publicity enticed the crowds to Wembley 'There they will be able to inspect the Empire from end to end . . . and see in each case the condition of life of the country they are visiting. That is the importance of the British Empire Exhibition. It is a stock-taking of the whole of the resources of the Empire'.

Visitors to this as yet unknown Middlesex were attracted by the great fun fair and the gardens attached to the exhibition. 'On summer nights, when the smell of the new-mown hay comes flowing into Wembley from all the fields around, and the stars are bright in a sky which knows no smoke fog, the wisest visitors of all will come to Wembley with no other object than to dine and saunter by the lakes, and see the fireworks, or play the happy fool in the amusement park'.

The exhibition opened again in 1925 and by the time it finally closed on 31 October, had been visited by some 27

million people. But it wasn't long before the place became a vast ghost city 'a vast white elephant, a rotting sepulchre of hopes and the grave of fortune'. The Stadium survived to become the home of sport and the crowds continued to use the GCR's two stations for the great sports events.

The effect of the exhibition was to open up this part of Middlesex as a desirable place in which to live. Within a decade the open fields around Wembley Hill, Sudbury and Sudbury Hill began to fill up with houses, shops and light industry.

The trams had reached 'The Swan', Sudbury in 1910, even though that part of the Harrow Road past Barham Park was still 'a narrow country lane, with hedges and greenwood on one side and a gravel path on the other'. Barham Park is at the side of the GCR embankment, approaching Sudbury and was the home of Sir George T. Barham, chairman of the Express Dairy Company. He had a model dairy

Sudbury Hill (Harrow)
A Marylebone express with Robinson GCR Class 5 locomotive, No. 5363. The year is 1937 and the houses in South Hill Grove (right) are still new. Their owners are enjoying their suburban life, with gardens full of roses, on the lower slopes of Harrow Hill.

Northolt Park

The locomotive on this LNER boat train bound for Immingham via the Chilterns(!) in 1938 is No. 5432 *Sir Sam Fay*. As Great Central locomotive No. 423, it featured in the old company's 1914 publicity handouts. Sir Sam, who lived to the great age of 96, became General Manager of the Great Central in 1902, and was knighted in 1912 by George V on the dockside at Immingham.

Opposite
The high noon of the Joint Line: Paddington bound express in 1938 with *King James II*.

in the grounds for many years. After his death the park was given to Wembley Council and now provides a pleasant area of green beside the railway.

Housing development at Sudbury village began in 1897, when the Conservative Land Company developed the old Harrowdene Estate. In the 1920s, the British Freehold Investment Company built Homefield Road and Priory Road near the Sudbury Station. Between Sudbury and Sudbury Hill there was quite a narrow area of land between the GCR line and the District Railway, and as early as 1910/15 two roads of terraced houses appeared on this site – Rosebank Avenue and Fernbank Avenue.

Sudbury Hill (Harrow) was originally name 'South Harrow & Roxeth' until 19 July 1926.

Developments at Northolt Park came in the mid 1930s. The station by the Northolt-Harrow Road was opened in May 1929, mainly to serve the new racecourse. In the following decade the course became very popular and the LNER in 1933 advertised cheap return fares from Marylebone at 7/6d (37½p),

3/9d (19p) and 2/5 (12p) including free entrance to the course. On big race days special trains were run. 'Only 15 minutes from Marylebone'.

There was little suburban development at Northolt Park and the adjacent area of Roxeth until the mid 1930s, when housing estates were laid out on the north side of the line. A new main road was constructed from Northolt Road through to Rayners Lane and named Alexandra Avenue in 1935 and Harrow Council saved an attractive wooded area of land for the public – Alexandra Park. Crossing narrow Field End Road about a mile beyond Northolt Park and the racecourse, the 'up' and 'down' lines run at different levels as they approach the well engineered fly-under junction at South Ruislip (Northolt Junction). It was only after the Second World War that light industry developed on the north side of the line. The housing developments, including the Victoria Park estate, began about 1938, but were not completed until after the War.

On the south side of the railway the country is still termed Green Belt.

58

The Growth of West London

FORWARD

Growth of West London

Turning now to the GWR line from Old Oak Common to Northolt Junction, development during the inter-war years was rapid, light industry and fairly densely built patches of inexpensive terraced and semi-detached housing. The GWR opened a number of halts between Old Oak Common and Greenford, but they hardly attracted much traffic.

At Park Royal, an important trading estate developed after the First World War. Here the GWR laid out extensive sidings which by 1956 were handling 246,000 tons of freight and 100,000 tons of coal. In 1968 a Freightliner Depot was built, and at least this part of the Birmingham line seems assured of freight traffic for some time to come. A halt was opened at Park Royal West on 26 September 1937 to provide a service for workers at the estate.

Before the building of the North Circular Road and the Western Avenue, the area remained open fields. There was a halt at Twyford Abbey from 1 May 1904 for seven years. The quiet countryside perhaps deserved a better fate than to be eventually half buried under factories, scrap yards and cheap housing. In *Highways and Byways of Middlesex* c1907, the author tells us of 'the pleasant walks one could do there: As we cross the stream here (the River Brent) a striking new railway viaduct cuts through the scene towards the Abbey. Great elms are being felled along the road leading to Hanger Hill, but the turning to the left to Twyford Abbey takes us through a long grove of tall trees, past the new

railway station. Hanger Hill is well timbered. The sloping grounds of Hanger Hill seem likely to be preserved for some time as they have been annexed by the golfing fraternity and easily afford one of the most beautiful links near London. To the east of the links, closely parallel with the railway cutting, is a real lane of thorns and brambles, passing along which to Twyford Abbey, we might think ourselves in the heart of the country.'

But already the shadows of the great developments to come were making themselves felt. In 'Rural London' the new railway was described as 'traversing . . . the ancient Perivale Forest and the uplands of Park Royal thus opening up a rural district for residential purposes'.

On Hanger Hill the Brentham estate was being laid out with high class housing in 1911.

The building of Western Avenue in the 1930s brought industry alongside the line at Perivale, including the descriptive 'art deco' landmark of the Hoover factory. The original halt at Perivale opened in 1904, but was replaced by a station in 1908. In the days before the GWR, Perivale was remote, despite Ealing being just over the hill to the south. And the village had its ghost:

'Unearthly sounds do still Prevail
But from no ghosts, alas!
They come from the GW Railway
When the express trains pass!'

It was a popular place for a day in the country and small parties of

Old Oak Common

The first stop on the new line out of Paddington was not far after the line left the old main tracks beyond the carriage sidings. Just coming to a stop on 24 June 1947 is GWR locomotive 5410 and an auto carriage on the local service to Greenford and Ruislip. The letter 'C' on the front of the locomotive is a duty code.

In the early 19th century Old Oak Common had been a Spa with 'water similar to Cheltenham'.

Greenford
GWR local trains were cut back to Greenford after the opening of the Central Line in 1947/48. Since then they have worked from Ealing Broadway to Greenford only and except in the rush hour, consist of a single diesel car.

North Acton
A Ruislip-bound local pulls into North Acton GWR station on 26 June, 1947. Note Boards – 'Alight here for electric trains to West End and City'. The lines to the right led to Wood Lane and the Kensington Olympia line along which trains came from the Southern Railway. Just through the more distant bridge, which carries the LMS to Richmond, is Old Oak Common Halt. The North Acton station opened in November 1923 and closed in 1947 when the Central Line was extended to Ruislip, although there was a Central Line station at Acton from the opening of the Ealing and Shepherd's Bush Railway in 1921.

Park Royal

This picture shows the station in May 1905. 'The importance of the first station, Park Royal, is much enhanced from its serving the Royal Agricultural Society's show ground', confided the *Transport and Tramroad Gazette* to its readers in the course of an article on the GW's new line (26 May 1905). The station had a siding directly into the grounds, a 700-foot loading bank, and a travelling crane among the many facilities to attract show traffic by railway. The station opened on 25 May 1903 and for many years there was a commemorative plaque in the booking hall reading: 'HRH The Prince of Wales travelled by the first train to carry passengers to this station. HRH was gracefully pleased to name this station "Park Royal".

Greenford

The original station about 1920 looking towards Northolt. The branch line train to Ealing is in the siding over to the far right. A goods train is being made up in the sidings near the Lyons factory.

Before Suburbia

Oldfield Lane, Greenford in 1912. No sign of the coming motor age and pavements, but a new housing estate was being planned on the left of the picture.

walkers would arrive at the small station, map in hand, to negotiate the field paths and climb the green slopes of Horsenden Hill. Fortunately those slopes have been preserved, and most remarkable of all, a wood beside the railway.

'The variable nature of the road is by no means of an unpleasant character, and at some distance along it we get to Perivale Halt, and pass under the arch of the GWR Wycombe and Birmingham Railway which breaks away from the main line at Acton . . . across to the right, over the open fields, the unfinished Wembley Tower may be seen showing its curious structure amid the surrounding trees'. (*Rambles Around Uxbridge* 1906).

Industry began at Perivale in the 19th century when Sir William Perkin set up his dye factory on a 6-acre site in 1857.

As late as November 1935, the developer of the Perivale Wood Estate advertised his houses as 'isolated from other estates . . . rural, yet only 5 miles from Marble Arch'. The Rockware Glass Company started operations at Perivale at the foot of Horsenden Hill in 1922 and 'houses for its workers are

being rapidly completed and occupied . . . another little colony is growing up'.(*Middlesex County Times* 10 July 1929).

Although the new station at Greenford was at first in open country, development began with The Greenford Freehold Land Company April 1911. They lavishly advertised the opening of their estate at Highview. 'The ideal site for an ideal home . . . the dawn of a new era. Although Greenford is virgin country, yet fully modern conveniences are available – telephone, telegraph, gas, electricity, water and company's mains.' Plots (25 x 35 feet) were available for as little as £5 deposit. Free railway tickets were offered and prospective buyers were informed that there was an 'excellent train service from Greenford Junction with a special increased train service for Easter'.

Even after 1919, there was plenty of open country at Greenford. A walks leaflet describes a ramble from Greenford to Horsenden Hill: 'A field path guide-posted "Sudbury and Horsenden" . . . is followed under the railway. Crossing the canal . . . the rambler carries on through the

Greenford

With the opening of the new line and the general improvement of transport service in the Ealing Borough area, various new housing projects were undertaken before 1914. In this view, bystanders loyally raise their hats as the Royal car passes the new Revenor Park Estate, Great Greenford. The fields, still dotted with hedgerow elms, have already been scarred for an estate road, while nearby, on the Highview Estate, houses were being offered with every inducement to city dwellers: 'Picture yourself amidst delightful rural surroundings, breathing pure air; watch your children romp in verdant pastures; and most important of all, imagine your proud feelings as you look at the land on which your castle is built and say THIS IS MY OWN PROPERTY.'

With the GWR's 'excellent train service . . . Greenford is by no means isolated . . . Paddington is reached in less than 15 minutes. The GCR offers a similar facility to Marylebone' (from Sudbury Hill, Harrow).

North Acton Junction 1946
A GWR goods train rumbles over the new concrete bridges beneath which the, as yet, unelectrified track has been laid for the Central Line extension to Greenford (and later Ruislip). A 1946 view.

Greenford
An Ealing Broadway to Greenford train takes the junction near West Ealing. The auto-trailer is No. 33 and the year of this picture is 1947. Today, the Greenford branch is worked by a diesel car, with another attached for peak hours. The last local service operated by the Western Region on the 'new' lines.

Building the Central Line

The Second World War is at last over and it is May 1946 as workmen begin to get things going again. A Paddington express passes by, and in the distance you can just see the formation for the flyover viaduct south of Greenford Station.

Greenford

The Underground is coming! The people who lived for miles around Greenford station were looking forward to the clean, swift tube trains that would take them straight to Oxford Circus or the Bank instead of the Great Western's smoky, oily old saloons with their sooty engines, to the vast caverns of Paddington!

Work in progress on the Central Line extension in May 1947. The tracks are down on the west bound road – but there seems still plenty to do before the opening in a month's time.

Old Northolt
Scene is what is shortly to become
Mandeville Road, by 'The Load of Hay'.
The year is about 1928 and the road
widening is just by the old Northolt Halt.

Opposite
Where London meets the country: You can
see the well-engineered route of the Joint Line
as it passes out of Middlesex and across the
gravel lakes and waterways of the Colne
Valley into Buckinghamshire.

The houses at the bottom left-hand corner
are in Ickenham. The house in the trees is
ancient Brackenbury Farm. Just up at the
left-hand side of the picture, where the black
air survey mark is, you can see Harvil Road
bridge, beyond which was situated South
Harefield Halt.

meadows and out to the "Ballot Box"
at the foot of Horsenden Hill. To the
right of the inn a path climbs up the
side of the hedgerow. There are
extensive prospects all around; to the
south the Surrey Hills mark the
horizon, with the Dorking Gap clearly
visible to the right of Ealing spire.'

But soon the trees and cows gave
way to light industry. Companies such
as J. Lyons set up factories, sidings
were laid out and the edges of
Greenford Green moved steadily
towards Northolt. The village of
Northolt, with its ancient church,
sparkling stream, cottages and a couple
of pubs was described in 1930 by
George Moss and Sons in their housing
advertisement as having 'A village
green, a beautiful old church, a little

moss-green churchyard, long vistas of
green fields where you can have your
home in the old rectory garden'.

The GWR halt opened on 1 March
1907. After the opening of the
Racecourse in 1929, there was a siding
for racehorse trains. The horses were
unloaded and led up a special ramp and
across a bridge built over the adjacent
Field End Road directly into the
racecourse. On big race days the GWR
ran special trains for race-goers.

The only other landmark was the
masts of the post office radio station,
opened on Petts Hill in 1930. It was
not until the building of the Western
Avenue (A40) in the late 30s that the
country changed to suburb. Even today
a wide sweep of open country divides
Northolt from Ruislip.

The New Commuterland

FORWARD.

The New Commuterland

When Northolt Junction station opened in 1908, one traveller reported that 'Here are still vast tracks of open country . . . and not a score of houses within a mile'.

The newly formed Ruislip-Northwood Council published elaborate plans for a garden city that was to include shops, a school and a church, as well as small 'workshops' near the Junction.

How remote and muddy the area must have seemed to the first travellers on the new railway! About the only buildings were those of Bourne Farm, home of the Smith family since the 17th century. The old Farmhouse (demolished about 1965) was reached by an elm lined trackway, which disappeared about 10 years later. It was a local businessman, Charles Hardy of Eastcote, who saw the potential for housing near the station. He formed The British Freehold Investment Syndicate with George Nesley and Masson Smith. 'Our aim is to buy land wholesale at the very lowest prices, and cut it up into plots and retail it at a reasonable profit', said the prospectus.

Local farmers were willing to sell the land, and so for £3 down and 50p a week one could begin to own a small plot of water-logged clay and grass beside the new railway at Northolt Junction. 'The suburbs have pure air, sunlight, roomy houses, grassy lawns.' Unfortunately, perhaps, many of the

purchasers found that they had to contact a builder and pay for him to build a home. So the earlier buildings were put up with sub-standard materials and the whole development was in danger of becoming a shanty town, without main drainage and services. The planning-conscious Ruislip Council was concerned. But then the First World War was to break out, silencing all local protests.

Afterwards, the original development Company became Home Freeholders and advertised: 'A freehold plot at Northolt Junction brings health, pleasure and profit'. Roads were named Great Central Avenue, Masson Avenue, etc. Shops were built along the muddy Station Approach. And some of the people who came to the air displays at the Northolt Aerodrome in West End Road were attracted by the countryside and bought plots. Others never found the money to build their dream home and patches of land remained vacant and weed-grown until fairly recent times.

It was the rapidly spreading estates promoted by the Metropolitan Railway's 'Metro-land' publicity that eventually pressed the GWR to heed to the RNUDC request for a halt by the bridge over muddy West End Road. Ruislip Gardens Halt opened on 9 July 1934 to serve George M. Ball's Manor Homes estate. This vast estate, with its grid plan of roads, began alongside the Metropolitan line at Ruislip Manor, but by the mid 1930s was spreading south

South Ruislip
Typical early British Railways scene on the Joint Line. A5 class LNER (former GCR) locomotive with a rake of teak carriages comes round the curve after passing under the GWR main line just south of the station

towards the Yeading brook. The Manor Homes Estate had an elaborate brochure which wooed Londoners: 'The ideal home is one that is set in the rural and unspoiled depths of the country and is yet accessible with ease, comfort and expediency from the heart of the City and West End. Come and see the palaces in miniature . . . at £450 freehold, repayment at 12/3d (61½p) per week.'

But attractive as the countryside seemed at Ruislip Gardens, the GWR's old fashioned auto-trailers and the LNER's sooty tank engines and rather musty teak carriages full of wealthy Bucks stockbrokers didn't really appeal to the lower paid clerks emigrating from Willesden, Ealing and other older parts of London to the green fields of bright new Ruislip Gardens. They preferred to walk the mile up to Ruislip Manor Station and travel on Frank Pick's bright new Piccadilly Line tube trains, or the Metropolitan's fast electric trains which took them right into the heart of London and not to some cavernous terminus such as Marylebone or Paddington. So Ruislip Gardens was hardly a very busy station, unless one worked in the factories of Greenford or Perivale. By the end of the 1930s Taylor Woodrow were advertising their bungalows alongside the Joint line for £485-625. And for your deposit of £25 you got the garden dug; and in the lounge, a fireplace with built-in radio and clock, and part of the moving expenses paid!

In March 1937 the *Middlesex Advertiser* (Uxbridge) reported 'new houses are rising daily whereas a year ago it had been open country'. A new parade of shops appeared complete with all the amenities of a fish and chip bar, an ironmonger's, Williams Brothers for the groceries and a neo-Tudor public house. Here was civilisation indeed!

Despite its location mid-way between the rapidly growing villages of Ickenham and Ruislip, the GWR station, with its goods yard and red brick buildings, did not attract much housing development in its immediate vicinity. Y.J. Lovell built some houses on the London side of the line in Ickenham Close before the First World War. It was during this conflict that the extensive depots of the RAF were built the other side of the Joint line. The depot on the south (or Ickenham) side was laid out along the land bounded by the Joint Line, and on the east, the Metropolitan. The contractors kept their horses in stables by the GWR station and one night there was a horrific fire which destroyed many of the beasts, despite the heroic efforts of the GWR stationmaster, Mr Lewis, to release them. The depot had connecting sidings from the main line. Most of the construction materials arrived by road, the solid-tyred military vehicles churning up the bad road surface, much to the concern of the villagers. The RAF depot on the Ruislip side consisted of a large number of barrack huts.

South Ruislip
Push-and-pull unit approaching the junction with the lines from Marylebone. The metal letter 'E' on the 0-6-0 GWR locomotive is a code. The signal box here is still in use and still has the name-plate 'Northolt Junction'.

Northolt Aerodrome

Not only was Northolt Junction given an inappropriate name for its location, but so was Northolt Aerodrome in West End Road. Even its site was possibly a mistake. Legend tells that the airborne surveyor was supposed to site the aerodrome on the Bourne Farm fields on the Harrow side of the Joint line, but had his map upside down! Certainly plans were announced for a flying field on the Bourne Farm site, to cover 256 acres and approached by a new 60-foot-wide avenue from the Junction. 'The Harrow Aerodrome . . . the Ranelagh of Flying . . . the Mecca of Aeronauts.' *The Morning Post* in 1912 stated that 'several hundred workmen are about to be turned to the task of removing the hedges and ditches'. But actually, nothing happened. The present airport began in January 1912 west of the Joint Line. This picture shows it just after the First World War (the first flight had taken place on 3 March 1915). The road at the bottom with the haycart is West End Road just by the railway. The Central Aircraft Company announced a grand victory pageant on 19 July 1919, with trains from London to Northolt Junction. 'View London's great peace day pageant from the air for £5.' In the Second World War the name of Northolt became immortal during the Battle of Britain. After the War, BEA flew many services from Northolt and it is now a busy military base.

South Ruislip

View of the old 'down' platform and entrance in 1937. The booking office in red brick was sited under the railway bridge on the 'up' side and remained until the 1960s. The old wooden platform buildings on the 'up' side were demolished in the 1970s.

The 'down' buildings and all the open land were swept away with the building of the Central Line.

Many of the weekend travellers on the line to Ruislip and Ickenham came to savour the delights of the various Ruislip pleasure grounds, including The Orchard Bungalow and The Poplars. To the south of the line, a few houses were built along the narrow High Road towards old Ickenham village. But there was little suburban development until the building of the Drummond Estate in 1923. The builders offered detached bungalows in quite large plots for £550 and one advertisement lured intending purchasers who had a sense of the historic with the legend that 'Queen Elizabeth picnicked under one of the oaks on the estate'. A row of shops, appropriately named Great Central Parade, was built on the Ickenham side of the station bridge in 1928.

All the countryside beyond Ickenham is now part of the London Green Belt. The flat Middlesex fields (once fringed by some very fine elms) give way to hilly country at the county border. The line passes through a deep cutting at Short Hill. Yet had it not been for the pre-War Green Belt Act, another London suburb would have spread itself over these high lands.

After 1919, the Harefield Place estate, home of the Newdigate family, and later Col. Cox, was put on the market. There was subsequently an ambitious plan for housing development, with shops and other amenities, including a country club in the old house and a golf course. Some development took place at the Uxbridge end of the estate. Again the builders lilted away: 'To those seeking a Residential Estate near enough to London to be handy, yet far enough away to be truly rural; an Estate whose modern efficiency happily mingles with old world charm, the Harefield Place Estate . . . fulfils every desire'.

The LNER agreed to build a halt at Harvil Road bridge just where the deep cutting opens out into the Colne Valley. But George Rose, the developer, had to guarantee the annual revenue from the halt for five years – amounting to £1,250 per year. Harefield halt opened on 24 September 1928 and included a short siding. 'The station is now open and 40 trains run daily to and from Paddington and Marylebone in 21 or 30 minutes.' The halt was approached by sloping inclines from the road bridge and the platforms were of wooden construction, with corrugated iron waiting shelters and a small booking hut on the 'up' side. The whole job cost £7,154.

In May 1929 the halt was renamed South Harefield Halt. But one fears that the duty booking clerk must have been a very lonely man. Hour after hour waiting for passengers that never came; staring out into the green fields and the canal or reading the *News Chronicle*. Sometimes there was a slight flurry of activity as a party of tired country walkers decided to call it a day and travel back from the halt, but few other people braved the miles of open road from either Harefield or Harefield Place estate to get a train. The booking office closed by 1930, although there were still 25 trains (17 on a Sunday).

There was yet another name change

South Ruislip
The confusion over the name 'Northolt Junction' lasted for many years. But eventually the Ruislip-Northwood Council persuaded the Joint Committee to alter the name to South Ruislip (although even today you can still read 'Northolt Junction' on the signal box!) A Marylebone bound express with B7 Class locomotive on 12 September 1932. At that time there was no development taking place north of the line.

South Ruislip
Described in 1926 by a local planner as 'A higglety-pigglety bungalow town' this picture of Station Approach about that time shows a variety of developments – including shops. As early as 1919 Home Freeholds saw a great future in South Ruislip: 'A freehold plot at Northolt Junction brings health, pleasure and profit.'

For years empty plots remained in roads such as Great Central Avenue, the original hopefuls who paid their deposit money have disappeared, probably because they could not afford to build the home of their dreams on the land.

South Ruislip July 1960
The finishing touches are being made to the Central Line Station in 1960, 12 years after the tube line opened.

Ruislip Gardens 1937
View of 'down' side with typical GWR 'pagoda' waiting shelters. Opened on 9 July 1934 to serve the rapidly developing local housing estates, the new amenity was not without local criticism. A letter to the local newspaper complained that 'Soon the pleasant fields will be yet another muddy, plan-less imitation of Rayners Lane, Ruislip Manor or Hillingdon'.

72

Ruislip Gardens 1948
Train on the opening day of the Central Line service – 21 November 1948. The station buildings are still only partly finished. The official opening train had in fact run from Greenford to West Ruislip the previous Friday. The GWR local service ceased from this date.

The GWR halt at the Gardens closed in 1958.

Ruislip Gardens 1949
Passing one of Geo. M. Ball's 'Manor Homes' (right) is a Marylebone train with Thompson 2-6-4T. On the left, the GWR locomotive (6142) is hauling an engineer's train.

Ruislip Gardens 1937

Across the fields, just visible on the left, is a large board advertising 'The Famous Manor Homes Estate Houses £450 to £765. Houses which have justifiably been described as 'palaces in miniature'. And all for only 12/6d (62½p) per week! But despite the amenity of the GWR halt, many of the new residents preferred the long walk to Ruislip Manor or Ruislip station and the 'safe, swift Underground of Mr Pick'. When this picture was taken Mr Shalford Ewer's farm just along the West End Road was said to be 'the last in that part of Ruislip', yet only a few years before it was in almost completely open country.

A King passes by . . .

After a gap of ten years, history was made in 1972 when preserved locomotive *King George V* passed by Ruislip Gardens with the Bulmers Cider train on the way to Olympia.

to simply 'South Harefield' in September 1931. But despite the eventual financial difficulties of Mr Rose, the developers were still advertising: 'A number of plots are available within 5 or 6 minutes' walk of Harefield Station of the GWR/GCR at £135 to £200 per foot frontage . . . Over 130 acres of lovely country is reserved for an 18-hole golf course, tennis courts and a freehold country house is reserved for club premises'.

One of the plans was to rename the road to Harefield 'Parkway'. The halt finally closed on 30 September 1931. However, its ghost was again seen when on the publication of the London Transport plan to extend the Central Line from North Acton out to Denham in 1936, there were proposals for a Harefield Road station on the same site. Perhaps it was all just as well for

the Green Belt that the Second World War came along. For today, there is still pleasant countryside here, with wide views to the Colne Valley on the west, and London in the East.

The branch line down to Uxbridge High Street which left the main line a short way beyond Harefield Halt was never a success and certainly did not influence any development. The fact that London passengers from Uxbridge had to change at Denham was a deterrent. Perhaps, had the Harefield Place plan gone ahead, there might have been an intermediate halt on the line. One can but speculate!

Denham village continued to sleep across the meadows from the new station until the mid 1930s, although the Rickmansworth and Oxford Roads were improved and widened around 1929/33.

Ruislip & Ickenham
The top picture shows the main entrance to the station about 1937. This was on the Ruislip (or 'up') side. In the station approach Mr Meacock had his estate agents' hut for many years and there were also 'Madame Eileen for ladies' hairdressing' and the grandly named 'Pinncolne Pari-Mutual turf accountancy'.

Ruislip & Ickenham
The other view is taken from the bridge on the Ickenham side. The approach road, buildings and footbridge all disappeared when the Central Line terminus was built on the land to the right after the Second World War. Three other points of interest: in the far distance along the track is the 'occupation' bridge that linked Primrose Hill Farm with its fields on the south side of the line. On the left of the picture is the stationmaster's house (demolished in the 1960s) and the houses of Ickenham Close, which were developed by Y.J. Lovell in 1913.

Ruislip and Ickenham
Steam up and ready to go to Paddington . . .
Local train with GWR 0-6-0T sandwiched
between two of the auto-trailers in the early
1930s. The trailer on the right is 49 of
1905, when she started life as a steam rail
car. Examine the chimney of the engine:
you can see a letter 'F', a code used for
various train duties.

Ruislip & Ickenham
Ending its days on a pick-up freight in the
1930s is this double-framed Armstrong
locomotive. The bridge was completely
rebuilt and the new station buildings erected
over the tracks when the Central Line was
extended after the Second World War.
   Let's hope it's not going to rain, as there
was very little weather protection on this
type of GWR engine.

Ruislip & Ickenham

It was the Metropolitan Railway which popularised Ruislip and 'Metro-land'. But some visitors came by the new Joint line and walked up the then wooded Ickenham Road. This picture of Old Ruislip was possibly taken by the GWR for use as a lantern slide or for display in carriage compartments.

On the left is the fence of Park House, then a row of cottages and shops, including Mrs Riddle's newsagents. 'The Swan' inn and at the end, Mr Crookall the butcher. The Old Post Office is the building with the massive chimneys in the middle of the picture. The young lady is cycling past the Police Station with its ornate lamp (now preserved in the modern police station nearby).

Ickenham

Just down the incline from the station was Great Central Parade, built in 1926 to serve the new estate of bungalows in The Greenway. The narrowness of the old road and the trees on the left remained at this point until as late as 1954.

Ruislip & Ickenham
A short walk up the Ickenham Road from the station and you came to Kings End Farm by the crossroads. Here, in the 1900s, George Weedon had his Sports Field and tea gardens – part of his Poplars Restaurant which stood in the centre of Old Ruislip. Children would come for miles by special trains to both the Metropolitan and the Joint station for a day at 'The Poplars'. In 1912 there was even a song written about it: 'Neath the shade of the Ruislip Poplars'.

Ickenham
The road to the station: The widening of High Road between the village and the Great Western Joint station radically changed the character of old Ickenham. This January 1934 scene shows how the boundary fence of the RAF depot (right) was set back, and the worst of the bend ironed out. On the left are some of the original post-1918 shops; Priors Garage; the Kennels at the end of Oak Avenue; the 'Soldiers' Return' public house; a row of Edwardian villas; then just visible through the bare winter trees the roof of Great Central Parade.

Ruislip & Ickenham
Approaching the station bridge, a Paddington express has just passed over the troughs. The water tank can be seen in the distance on the left.

Ickenham

The road to the Joint station and Ruislip seen from the pump and pond in about 1932. The public house in the centre of the picture is the original 'Fox and Geese', with the old village school beyond. Although the pond and Home Farm remain, the school and pub went with the widening of the road between 1933 and 1934.

Ruislip and Ickenham

Work is well advanced in this 1948 picture of the new Central Line terminus. The old GWR footbridge is still in position, but the 'down' waiting room has been rebuilt. The non-electrified track on the far left led to the RAF depot. It is now used for London Transport stock deliveries and for departing rolling stock en route to the breakers' yard in the Midlands.

Ickenham

'Situated off the beaten track, and far from the encroachments of any railway, Ickenham village little changes from year to year . . . and remains one of the most rural of our Middlesex villages.' Well that was how it was in 1895, a few years before this peaceful scene. The pump was a gift of Charlotte Gell in 1866. Fortunately both the pump and church still remain amid modern shopping parades.

Ruislip and Ickenham
Lift off! Once the Central Line station had advanced sufficiently with buildings and connecting bridge to the GWR station, the old bridge became redundant. So on 30 June 1947 it was removed, although the Central trains did not commence running until 21 November 1948

Ruislip and Ickenham
View looking west, with one of the Blue Pullman sets rushing under the bridge and on towards Paddington in September 1963. Ruislip Golf Course is on the right, and the steam locomotive is GWR 2-6-2T No. 6132. Later she shunted over to the far left siding to pick up the new tube stock and tow it into the London Transport depot south of the station ready for final fitting out before it was sent to run on the Piccadilly Line. The last Blue Pullman ran through Ruislip on regular service on Saturday 4 March 1967.

Ruislip and Ickenham

Where London meets the country: You can see the well-engineered route of the Joint line as it passes out of Middlesex and across the gravel lakes and waterways of the Colne Valley into Buckinghamshire.

The houses at the bottom left-hand corner are in Ickenham. The house in the trees is ancient Brackenbury Farm. Just up at the left-hand side of the picture, where the black air survey mark is, you can see Harvil Road bridge, beyond which was situated South Harefield Halt.

Ruislip and Ickenham

In the 1960s the 'Western' diesels were a familiar sight on the expresses through Ruislip. This picture was taken from the Ickenham road bridge in 1962.

The suburb that never was
'An unspoiled beauty spot only 25 minutes from London . . . surrounding the new South Harefield Station' is how the estate brochures advertised George Rose's proposed housing estate on the extensive Harefield Place estate. The lands, originally owned by the Newdigate family, had been up for sale several times after the death of the last owner of the great house. The plans for shops, villas and bungalows failed to attract buyers except at the Ickenham-Uxbridge end. 'The new South Harefield Station from which Marylebone and Paddington will be reached in 25 minutes, is right in the centre of the estate', said the literature optimistically.

A board announces the opening of the station. But traffic never came and, soon after, the Green Belt was formed

South Harefield
Another evocative shot of the 'High Noon' period on the Joint Line. It is 1938 and 6017 *King Edward IV*, built in 1928, speeds along for Paddington. This locomotive worked until July 1962.

South Harefield
It's a sunny afternoon in 1938 as *King Henry VII*, fitted with a modified bullet-nose shaped smokebox, speeds the 9.10 am to Birmingham. The well-dressed lady looking out of the window is probably thinking that her newly-acquired husband ought to buy one of those bright new suburban houses she has seen back down the line at Ruislip Gardens.

South Harefield
Twenty years and a World War later: LNER B1 class locomotive with a mixed assortment of carriages, passes along Short Hill cutting on the long journey to Sheffield.

Uxbridge
'Good Pull In', says the sign outside the old GWR terminus at the bottom of Uxbridge High Street in this September 1929 picture. The Oxford Road ran past the station and already the railway was feeling the effects of road competition. When the station opened in May 1907, there were girders right across the road in anticipation of the line being taken round the outskirts of the town with the Vine Street station. Uxbridge was so proud of its new link in 1907 that Lucy and Birch, the local printers, produced a commemorative postcard. The first station-master was a Mr Carpenter who had originally been at Hungerford. In 1922 the bridge over High Street was removed and whilst the girders were being winched down, some of the workmen nearly became entangled with the chains.

Uxbridge

The last passenger train for Denham left in 1939 as war broke out. But services on the branch had been in decline ever since the GWR finally decided not to proceed with the continuation over High Street to Vine Street. In the First World War the branch was closed because of 'light traffic' and a bus ran from Denham to Uxbridge.

The tracks were removed for use in France and after the War only one line was relaid. Goods traffic lingered until 1964. This picture of the ruins of the wooden station dates from 1954.

Uxbridge

This picture shows what is believed to be the very last train working in the sidings on 16 January 1964. The locomotive is a 2-6-2T No. 5564. The goods and coal depot closed in July 1964, and all track has now been removed. Part of the old formation of the branch has been bulldozed away to form part of the Colne Valley Nature Park.

Uxbridge

'The building of this station will undoubtedly form an important part of the extensive railway enterprise in this district which has opened up such promising areas in both Middlesex and Buckinghamshire. Uxbridge will now, at least tentatively, have a more convenient communication with the districts of Denham, Ruislip, Northolt and Greenford.' The building of the branch down to High Street from the main line was greeted with enthusiasm in Uxbridge. In this picture preliminary work is under way for clearing the site ready to build up the short viaduct on which the future station is to be built. In the background is the giant plane tree, over 200 years old, which had to be chopped down. The felling took place at 12.30 pm on 13 July 1906.

Uxbridge

Approaching Uxbridge High Street station in September 1954: one of the GWR diesel railcars working a special train. The water tower in the background was unusually sited some distance from the platform ends.

Opposite

The Joint Line runs through some superb scenery between West Wycombe and Saunderton. Here on a lovely Sunday morning towards the end of the steam era a local train steams up the 1 in 164 gradient with the 9.45 am Aylesbury to High Wycombe.

Amid the Chiltern Beeches

FORWARD.

Amid the Chiltern Beeches

One day a famous film producer saw an advertisement for the sale of 'The Fisheries', an old house with 225 acres of land beside the river Colne at Denham. The man was Sir Alexander Korda, and this was what he was looking for to build new studios for London Films. Here was good transport and attractive surroundings. Backed by loans from the Prudential Assurance Company, he hired Hollywood studio designer Jack C. Okley to help him create his great dream palace – the 'British Hollywood'.

During 1935/36 the fields north of the Joint railway were a centre of great activity, as 1,000 men worked on the construction of the studios, which were to cover a 26-acre site, and even included a small power station. The main studios were finished with grey walls and green roofs to blend with the wooded surroundings. Despite the setback of a fire during construction, the studios began their first films even before the complex was completed.

The years up to 1939 were exciting times at Denham Studios. Its name became world famous. Films such as *The Shape of Things to Come, Sanders of the River, The Private Life of Henry VIII,* as well as Britain's first colour film, *Wings of the Morning,* were made here. The great architect, Walter Gropius, was commissioned to design (in 1936) the world's most modern film processing laboratories adjacent to the studio site. These were the days when you could see some of the most famous film stars in the world dining together in the Denham Studios restaurant. They would come along the main road, some by chauffeured cars

Denham
The Grand Union Canal Viaduct: 'A very fine piece of bog and water bridging, the canal arch of the elliptic form being of grand proportions and the whole cluster of arches of weather-defying blue-brick . . . producing an imposing effect.' (*Rambles Round Uxbridge* 1914).

Denham
When this turn-of-the-century picture was taken, the villagers were viewing with fear and apprehension the pending arrival of vast armies of navvies and all the mess of building the new railway just north of the village.

from the station – people like Charles Laughton; Marlene Dietrich; Edward G. Robinson and 'Schnozzle' Durante; Gertrude Lawrence; Merle Oberon; Robert Donat – the list was endless.

In the 1940s came films about contemporary life, with *The First of the Few; In Which We Serve; Blithe Spirit; Morning Departure;* and *Hamlet.* But by 1951 Walt Disney was making *Robin Hood* – the very last full film made at Denham. There was a decline in the industry and the famous studios became warehouses, sound studios and at one time the American Military had a base there.

Now the great structures with their memories are gone. The site has been cleared for light industrial development, although the processing laboratories remain. In July 1936 the GWR began purchasing land for the proposed Central Line Terminus and just before the War, the first shopping parades arrived. But fortunately Denham never really developed as an outer London suburb.

Denham Golf Club halt, complete with characteristic GWR Pagoda waiting shelters opened in July 1912 and was busy during World War I, when there was a large army camp in the vicinity. In 1923 the Pitcher Construction Company announced plans for houses at what is now called High Denham, but it was to be the 1930s before commuters outnumbered golfers using the halt. Higher up on the hills, Denham Flying Club established itself, and on a summer day in the 1930s a typical sound as an LNER local steamed into the halt, was the buzz of a Tiger Moth crossing the blue sky, high above the silver birches.

Denham
The new railway is coming and the pubs in peaceful Denham village were abuzz with gossip and the latest scandals about the activities of the Navvies. But they are all hard at work here getting Denham ready for the laying of the four railway tracks. There was a plan to call the station 'Denham Street'. In March 1915 these platforms were to be packed to capacity with the men of the 16th Bn. King's Royal Rifles as they left their local camp for the Front. Many were the heavy hearts and wet eyes as the local womenfolk turned out to say farewell. For too many, it was to be goodbye.

Denham

A train for Birkenhead passes through the station on the fast tracks. The engine is *King Henry IV* which at the time of this June 1956 picture, was located to Wolverhampton (Stafford Road) shed. Denham signal box closed in June 1975, although the centre lines were taken up in the mid-1960s. In early Joint Line days some special expresses stopped here from Marylebone. In 1922 a Grand National Race Special was advertised. For a 1st Class return fare of £3.5s (£3.25p) you could have a day at the Race course – and have lunch and dinner on the train as well!

Denham

The Shape of Things to Come: Sir Alexander Korda's Palace of Dreams under construction in 1936. Thousands of men worked on the 28-acre site from 1935/36 to build his London Film Studios and even before they had finished, the films were in production.

Denham golf club

Originally opened as a 'Platform' in August 1912, the Denham Golf Club became a halt. Apart from the Golf Course, there was little else here until about 1936, although the Pitcher Construction Company announced plans in 1923 for a housing estate and shops on the site of the wartime army camp. Up on the hill above the station is the Airfield where parachutists were trained in the Second World War.

The train in this 1956 picture is No. 5010 '*Restormel Castle*'.

Crossing the Misbourne

When the viaduct over the Misbourne valley and the road from Tatling End to the Chalfonts was completed in 1905, the *Morning Leader* carried pictures and an article praising its well-laid bricks and design: 'The stations, too, are on the most modern lines.'

The train steaming across in this December 1960 picture is in charge of an ex-LMS 2-6-4T and the days of Marylebone suburban steam are drawing to a close.

Gerrards Cross

Two 1912 views at this rather unusual station. Unusual because the booking office is on the first floor of the 'up' platform buildings! This is due to the depth of the cutting here and the gradient of the slope to the main road.

In our first picture, GWR steam railcar No. 98, built in February 1908, is waiting to leave for either Paddington, or Denham and round the branch to Uxbridge High Street. These cars seated 61 people: 36 in the non-smoking saloon and 16 in the smoking. The other seats were for the unlucky latecomers, who had to sit with the parcels!

The GWR steam railcars were curious vehicles. They were basically a long carriage, with an 8-foot Dean bogie on which was mounted a vertical steam boiler. Apparently, apart from making the carriage rather sooty and dusty it was hot as well in the summer. Even the driver and fireman disliked working with them and, in fact, the firemen preferred to adjust and fuel the firebox at stations, as they were afraid of what might happen when the monster was boiling along at speed! Eventually the steam boilers were removed and the saloons converted into auto-trailers for working with tank engines.

When this picture was taken, a season ticket cost £3.1s 0d (£3.05p) to London and the local rates were 4s (20p) in the £.

Gerrards Cross
The Joint Line at War. Scene in about 1915
with a Great Central Ambulance train
running through on its journey from the
Channel Ports to the safety of the Midlands.

Gerrards Cross
No expenses were spared when they built
the new line through the Chilterns. Passing
tracks at local stations and high graceful
bridges. This 1947 picture shows the
generous proportions of Joint Line stations.
The train of ex-GCR stock is leaving for
Marylebone behind a Thompson 2-6-4.

Out-of-Town Housing Schemes

Of all the places along the Chiltern section of the line, it was at Gerrards Cross and Beaconsfield where the most development took place. Indeed, the Joint line created entirely new towns at both places, the original settlements being situated along the Oxford Road.

April 1910 saw the start made on the Latchmore Estate at Gerrards Cross, the developer, J.C. Richards, calling the district 'The Brighton of Bucks'. At one time it was also described as 'A highly respectable and genteel place'.

Kirkham, Burgess and Myers advertised the Orche Hill estate: 'Excellent freehold building sites', whilst Percy A. Hopkins advertised The Milton Park Estate which 'occupies the choicest position on the outskirts of this district. Houses will be built to suit tenants' requirements or would be sold freehold or leasehold'.

The emphasis was on high class houses, spacious grounds and rural peace 'combining country life and town convenience . . . 22 minutes from Marylebone'. Even as late as 1927, Gerrards Cross was very class conscious and a guide book stated: 'It is one of the features of the district that all the good class property is grouped in one part and the artisan type in another'.

Shops soon grew up at the top of the long slope from the station, but one incongruous feature for so high-class a place was the opening, in 1911, of a roller-skating rink. It was open every evening from 7 pm till 10 pm. Admission was 6d (2½p), with an additional 6d (2½p) for roller skating on the Rock Maple Floor. Seer Green and Jordans halt opened on New Year's Day 1915, no doubt to give war-weary golfers a chance on the links and perhaps an indication of how lightly the War was taken at first. The halt was in fact named 'Beaconsfield Golf Links' until 1918. This was in the heart of

Milton and William Penn country and the halt where pilgrims to Jordans and Chalfont St Giles alighted to see the Mayflower barn, the old Quaker Meeting House (1688), and perhaps the simple plot where Penn, founder of Pennsylvania, lies. This is typical Chilterns countryside, with its superb beech trees and narrow lanes, where in old times primroses could be found in Spring.

In 1919 work began here on a garden village designed by Fred Rowntree. In 1929 another carefully hidden estate was built at Jordans, with houses on ¼-acre plots 'in some of the best scenery in the county . . . which is being developed so as to preserve the amenities of the Friends and the Meeting House'. However, there were some ugly signboards by the station.

A hundred acres of land was eventually preserved as open space near the station. In the end, housing developments were very well planned

and are mainly hidden from the railway. In fact, the plantations of evergreens and silver birches make this one of the most attractive spots on the line.

The early railway traveller to Beaconsfield could take tea at 'The Railway Hotel' where Mrs Borglase ran a 'good class family and residential hotel', or could walk the mile up the hill to the old town, with its wide main street, lovely church and numerous inns and tea rooms.

Edmund Burke, the 18th-century statesman who entertained Dr Johnson and Mrs Thrale at his Beaconsfield home, had one of the first estates developed named after him: 'Burke's Estate, covered 300 acres, with sites for bungalows or freehold houses near the station for £1.13s.2d (£1.66p). There is an excellent service of trains to and from London . . . the journey occupying about 35 minutes.' the advertisements crooned.

Beaconsfield
Before the Joint line was built, passengers for Paddington or Wycombe had to travel to the nearest railway station at Wooburn Green, some three miles distant down steep hills. The GWR eventually started a motor bus service all the way to the main line at Slough and here it is about to start out from the Yew Tree in 1904. The safety conscious or nervous passenger no doubt glanced with apprehension at the primitive brakes that only acted on the rear wheels!

In 1908 this service was extended to Windsor

The locomotive is a Thompson 4-6-0, No. 61136, with a train of milk empties coming up from outer Buckinghamshire on 10 July 1955.

Seer Green & Jordans

Opened as Beaconsfield Golf on New Year's Day 1915 (presumably to cheer up war weary golf fans): this halt became Seer Green & Jordans in January 1918. The club house stands beside the 'down' platform and is a suburban villa style. On the north side of the line a dense plantation of firs, beeches and silver birches shield the carefully-sited villas. A mile down the road is Jordans village. In 1929, one writer complained about the builders' hoardings here, but eventually good planning prevailed.

Seer Green & Jordans

The countryside in this part of Buckinghamshire is associated with the early Quakers, including William Penn, as well as the poet John Milton. A guide book to Seer Green and Jordans issued in 1911 says that the area is 'easily reached by means of the GCR . . . a delightful district easy of access from Gerrards Cross station'. The halt at Seer Green opened in 1915. The locomotive here is L1 Class 2-6-4 with a train of LNER articulated carriages on the Marylebone local service.

Beaconsfield

The First World War was still two years
ahead and the man with the fashionable
straw boater and the complicated looking
luggage is no doubt looking forward to a day
in Oxfordshire with his friends, and tea at
the Rectory with the Curate.

Beaconsfield

Outside the new station, seen here in about
1910, you could catch Frank Bowler's
'door to door' service. He would wait for the
regular passengers so that they wouldn't
miss their trains to Marylebone!

You could also have your heavy luggage
brought down to the station (or taken home
after the seaside holiday) by Mr Young,
who was known as 'The outside porter' –
which title he proudly displayed on his
barrow! Later he became a fishmonger and
would get his fresh supplies from the early
morning 'down' train. The locals then called
him 'Old Young'.

Beaconsfield

The new town could boast of shops, banks
and pavements by the early 1920s, although
herds of cattle were still frequently seen!
Even as early as 1910, a Reading Room
was open for the entertainment of the new
suburban residents. 'Open 10 am to 11 pm
to residents on payment of a small fee.'

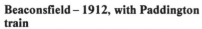

Beaconsfield – 1912, with Paddington train
Getting to Beaconsfield Station from the more outlying parts of the town was easy if you got Sid Williams' bus. He would even stop outside your house if he knew you. The route started from 'The White Hart Hotel' in the Old Town. By the 1920s the bus was mechanised and run by Frank Bowler.

Beaconsfield
An unusual view taken on 29 July 1956 when LBSCR H2 Class locomotive No. 32425 *Trevose Head* steamed through the rain with a ramblers' special from far away East Croydon. One wonders how they all survived the weather when they got to their destination in the Chilterns. The locomotive was withdrawn a month later.

Beaconsfield was said to have the lowest infant mortality rate in Buckinghamshire . . . and the town 'does not suffer from the dampness and mist so prevalent in the neighbouring districts'. To endorse this rather dubious statement, one local estate agent said that a number of well-known surgeons had come to live in the area!

Perhaps the most famous of the residents in the early years was G.K. Chesterton, the novelist and poet, who lived at 'Top Meadow' in Grove Road from 1912 to his death in 1935. He was a well-known passenger on the GWR/LNER and few could fail to miss him, in his flowing cape and broad-brimmed hat. One thing he was techy about – the correct

pronounciation of the town's name 'Beck-ons-field'. A story asserts that he once held up the crowds at Marylebone ticket barrier whilst he politely, but in a loud voice, corrected the ticket man! he even wrote a verse:

'To us our town, to fling
Wide as its roads and white
That all men may pronounce it good
And some pronounce it right.'

Beaconsfield for many years marked the end of the commuter belt. High Wycombe has always been a town in its own right, with busy small industries – particularly furniture. Much of the modern housing around the town is a product of the Post-War years. Today

its station is busy with commuters heading for London, whilst the 'down' platform becomes packed around 8.20 in the mornings with hundreds of schoolchildren and students coming into the town for education.

Princes Risborough began to grow a little in the 1930s and there are some more recent housing estates, but there has been nothing like the growth that occurred on the Metropolitan-Great Central Joint Line. North of Princes Risborough, the GWR opened a series of halts to attract people away from the local bus services. The halts included Ilmer (1.4.29); Dorton (21.6.37); South Aylesbury (10.2.33); and on the Watlington branch: Wainhill Crossing (1.8.25).

Beaconsfield
Last years of steam on the Joint line saw some of the classic GWR express locomotives on fairly mundane duties. Here *Swansea Castle* stops at Beaconsfield with a rush hour Paddington to Banbury train in August 1963. She was built in 1928 and ran until 1964.

Altering the track layout on the approaches to High Wycombe
This interesting photograph taken during the days when the original High Wycombe to Risborough Railway, a creature of the Great Western, was being incorporated into the more demanding role of the GW & GC Joint Line. Although much of the hard work had already been done, it was necessary to widen the whole approach and form embankments. Already a new bridge has been constructed in the background and much spade work remains. The old Western style track will soon be lifted. This scene is west of High Wycombe station.

Reconstruction near High Wycombe (1)
The picture shows the bleak winter scene as the original single-track line, upon massive embankments, curves tightly to cross a brick viaduct into the town of High Wycombe, before the Joint Line had arrived. The time is 1902, and the early Great Western track, with its occasional transverses and centre pit cut a distinctive pattern. New housing is under erection on the left of the photograph.

Reconstruction near High Wycombe (2)
The contractors have, in the second photograph, lifted the old track and infilled considerably to allow new train sidings to be built. The viaduct arches and abutments are in the process of being refaced and relined to carry high-speed trains. A large stack of prepared railway sleepers await the arrival of the railway platelayers.
Opposite, top

Reconstruction near High Wycombe (3)
As the works approach completion, the scene reverts to a calm ordered railway, now with double tracks leading to the reconstructed viaduct.
Opposite, lower

The works at High Wycombe Station
This photograph shows the original track layout just west of the High Wycombe station platforms and the work gangs assembled to remove the old 'Western' style metals. It was necessary to rebuild much of the ancillary buildings at the station, including the original signal box and the massive retaining wall, to be seen beyond the steel bridge. The footbridge can also be seen in illustration.

Locomotive 7808 at work between High Wycombe & Beaconsfield
A special from Snow Hill on 7 September 1966. The old Western 4-4-0, in drab British Railways livery, still manages to look remarkably clean in this very late scene.

Mr Keen's road show hits the trail

Here, with the whole of High Wycombe, it seems, up and ready to watch the occasion, is an early competitor of the railways – a steam lorry capable of carrying some very heavy loads. Those of us old enough to remember the steam lorry will recall the rather awful presence they made upon passers-by. William Keen, a local haulier, welcomes the return of the first steam lorry from London, in 1904. The journey time was 74 hours for a return trip, compared with the 12 days of a horse-drawn waggon-load.

It must have been an extremely uncomfortable journey trundling along in an atmosphere of steamy heat on iron wheels. The loads were furniture for the London markets.

Steam coaches had been seen on the roads since the 1830s, but the sparks, noise and fire from these monsters were enough to frighten horses and to cause them to be very restricted in the country.

Last trip of the 'opposition'

This three-horse bus, the last horse bus in the district, stands outside the 'White Blackbird' public house at Loudwater, High Wycombe, ready for the very last trip. It was the passing of the age of the horse bus, the early competitor of the railway. After the war, at this time only a year away, the motor bus was soon to show its flexibility in serving small country communities. The vehicle, owned by the local High Wycombe firm of Livery & Posting, has Driver Axton, well guarded against the worst of the weather, with reins in hand.

A little mystery at High Wycombe

A rather satisfied group of railway officials and workmen appear in this official-looking picture at High Wycombe during work in connection with the new Joint Line.

Mr Woods, of the High Wycombe Historical Society, notes that the signal box in the picture is not the one built after the rebuilding of the station and that none of the officials or navvies appear in other official pictures taken of the new railway by Mr S.W.A. Newton. Although there are grounds for disagreement, it may be that this scene was taken near Gordon Road.

Construction poles (which were made in those days from wood) can be seen in the course of erection near the signal box on the right, which could help to date this as around 1901/02.

High Wycombe

The forecourt, before the age of the motor car, with broughams and a horse-and-trap awaiting passengers from the London Train. The main poster display along the front of the station is divided equally between the Great Western and Great Central advertising. Notice the odd shape of the station chimneys.

High Wycombe

Heroes' return: The triumphant arrival of the Buckinghamshire Yeomanry at High Wycombe, May 1901. The Yeomanry had seen some reverses in the South African War, and were at the Relief of Lindley, and the taking of Bethlehem, in the Orange Free State. It was the 'high noon' of Britain's Imperial Age, and the swirl of patriotic fervour caused men and boys to clamber on the goods waggons and carts in the freight yard for a grandstand look.

The procession was led by the Fire Brigade, resplendent in gleaming brass, and the local bandsmen playing the air of 'See the Conquering Hero comes', with great gusto. While the brave whistles of the locomotives in the station added to the excitement, an eye-witness wrote:

'It was this war which revealed the alarming malnutrition amongst the recruits from the rural areas. Poverty was seen, for the first time, as contributing to 'the decline of the nation'.'

The original station is seen here. When the Joint line was built a few years later, the footbridge was removed and the 'up' platform (you can just see the chimney of its buildings on the left) was rebuilt further along the line, beyond the water tower.

Char-a-banc party in High Wycombe, c1923

Competing with the railways for excursion traffic, the motor coach (or char-a-banc) which had been developed rapidly after the First World War had two features in its favour – cheapness and novelty. The people who formed these early coach parties were hardy souls, riding very exposed to the worst of the weather, although actual downpours of rain were dealt with by a collapsible hood that took a considerable time to get into place and seriously reduced viewing. But the char-a-banc parties (and here the passengers are being given a potted history of High Wycombe with the aid of a tin megaphone) were able to stop at will at local inns along the way home – a clear advantage over railway excursions.

High Wycombe
As well as Birmingham, expresses worked through to Birkenhead and some of the locomotives, such as Star Class *Glastonbury Abbey*, were based at the Shrewsbury depot.

This picture dates from June 1957.

High Wycombe
A wide variety of freight stock can be seen on this goods train approaching High Wycombe in 1947.

High Wycombe

Wrong road running: This unusual railway operating scene was taken by the old High Wycombe Middle Box (closed 1972) in the late 1950s. 'Hall' Class No. 4941 *Llangedwyn Hall*, is overtaking an LMS Fairburn Tank locomotive No. 42281. The 'Hall' is on a Paddington express and the LMS engine a train to Marylebone. The Marylebone train is waiting for the express to clear the station so that it can cross over to the 'up' platform.

High Wycombe

Modern image: One of the 'Blue Pullman' diesel sets approaching the Paddington platform in July 1963. The Pullman trains ran between Paddington and Wolverhampton from 1960 until March 1967. In 1964 the 1st Class ordinary return fare from London all the way was £3.50p plus 50p supplement (or £2.35 plus 25p 2nd). The menu, with meals served at every seat, included smoked salmon at 37½p; grilled sole and chips 62½p; cold buffet 42p and the coffee (in china cups) 3½p!

Twilight days at West Wycombe *Above*
West Wycombe station suffered in later
years in its struggle for local passengers
from the local fast bus service competition.
The station closed on 3 November 1958.

This scene, in October 1956, shows the
'Hall' Class 4-6-0 locomotive *Guildhall*
5927 heading the Birmingham-Paddington
express. This locomotive was allocated to
Tyseley (Code 84E) and was built at
Swindon in June 1933. It was withdrawn in
October 1964.

Pride takes a fall
The unhappy ending to a motor car trip at West Wycombe in 1907. In Edwardian days the motor car was essentially for local use; most people came from London by train, even the rich and famous like the author, G.K. Chesterton, whose home was at Beaconsfield. This car had brake failure after a heavy burst of speed along the straight stretch of road in the background, and failed to make the bend. The chauffeur appears in the small crowd while a top-hatted dignitary, perhaps the passenger in the car, gives the boy, astride the horse which is to pull the vehicle clear, some earnest instructions. A woman witness felt that 'these dangerous monsters should be confined to iron rails!'

West Wycombe – 1904 *Left*
A typical village street scene when the 'Acton & High Wycombe Railway' was being built. Many of the buildings are unkempt (as compared to West Wycombe today under the protection of the National Trust). The children stand in an untidy line across the road. Behind, a two-horse bus, the competitor of the new railway in the area, waits to begin its journey into town. The large oval sign that hangs from the building on the left marks the 'George & Dragon' inn – a 14th-century hostelry which has a famous ghost. This is Susan, an inn servant in mortal life. She died, so the legend runs, outside West Wycombe caves one night after falling back in terror and striking her head upon a stone following a foolish prank played upon her by the village locals. Susan advertises her present by dramatically reducing the temperature in the room in which she intends to 'work' that evening

Rabbit pie *(Top)*

Two little country boys with the family's
haul of harvest rabbits. In the same way
that country gentry liked to display their
prowess with a 'bag' of game birds, so the
country labourers looked forward to a large
catch of rabbits at harvest time. Gangs of
children, with sticks and clubs, waited in
each cornfield as the reaper-binder moved
in circles towards the centre and the last
stand of uncut wheat. Then, as the last
refuge was cut, the wretched rabbits and
other wildlife broke in desperation for the
far away hedges. Most were clubbed to
death. This haul, already gutted, could
easily have lived in just one field of corn,
and meant rabbit pie for weeks for farming
families.

Country cornfield *(Lower)*

Chilterns cornfield in high summer, 1910.
'We followed the pleasant footpath that
begins to the right of Bradenham church and
finishes short of Hughenden Park.
West Wycombe station was not a great
distance away.'

West Wycombe, 1964

An 'up' pick-up coal train, hauled by 61XX
Class 2-6-2 tank No. 6167, just beyond the
abandoned West Wycombe station on 26
September 1964. The church, surmounted
by the famous 'Golden Ball' (actually a
small room reached by a ladder from the
church tower) dominates the hill in the
background.

In the years after the First World War,
the ' Golden Ball' was a tourist attraction of
even greater difficulty than the top gallery in
St Paul's. The visitor had a flimsy vertical
ladder to climb from the tower of the church
to enter the Ball chamber vertically above
the head. It was especially risky for ladies,
and on windy days! In the chalk hill below
the church are the West Wycombe caves,
The Hell Fire Club, in Georgian days, were
said to 'practise' strange rites in these
subterranean caverns. They included Sir
Francis Dashwood, who built a straight
road to High Wycombe from the village,
and the Earl of Bute, who employed Robert
Adam to build his house at Luton Hoo. Of
the church, with its splendid position
overlooking the road and later the railway,
the wit Charles Churchill wrote that it was
'a temple set aloft in air, that serves for
show and not for prayer'.

The Sunday School Treat

Those Wesleyan Church treats at High Wycombe', recalled one old country lady, Mrs Foster, 'they were really grand affairs for us boys and girls, and for the teachers who were smartly decked out in their finest hats and dresses. It always seemed so hot in those days. We would go out of High Wycombe on a great train of waggonettes, everybody waving wildly, while the local Band of Hope sometimes turned out and played so loudly that I remember the horses appearing very frightened by the noise.' Outings sometimes used local trains: 'we didn't go far.' Places such as Burnham Beeches were thought too distant for the day's outings. 'Lots of lemonade and food we had', she added wistfully.

Lining Saunderton cutting
The scene in 1905, as teams of navvies labour on the final smoothing work on the walls of Saunderton cutting working with picks whilst suspended by ropes looped around their middles. Below, at the foot of the cutting, newly creosoted sleepers are chaired and await rails.

Saunderton over 50 years later:
Birmingham bound train with Castle Class 7010 'Avondale Castle' in June 1958. On the left is the 'up' line rising out of the cutting.

Speeding through the Chilterns
A Wolverhampton bound express in July
1958 with 'King' Class No. 6014 *King
Henry VII*. In 1935 this locomotive,
together with No. 5005 *Manorbier Castle*
were treated to some streamlining
experiments which gave them a very odd
appearance. Gradually the streamline
panels were removed.

Saunderton station
Nostalgic scene one sunny day in July
1957. It was very unusual to have an
express train stop at this wayside station.
The locomotive is *King George II*. There's
engineering work on the line and the
pilotman is walking towards the footplate to
join the crew for the slow trip forward
towards Princes Risborough.

  Look at all the parcels waiting shipment,
even on this small country station.

Saunderton
The clock has turned back to 1938. The war clouds are gathering, but Mr Chamberlain thinks things will turn out alright. The passengers on the Wolverhampton express watch the peaceful downland scenery go by as *King James II* takes them home to the Midlands.

The village people as 'extras'
Potential passengers of the new railway, as though aware they have been hurried into a new fast world of steam railways with London on their doorsteps, wait in jaunty positions for their picture to be taken. Behind them, the ancient Whiteleaf Cross rises over the chimneypots, cut into the steep 45° slope that forms a back drop at the village. It is of uncertain origin, perhaps a Christian 'clean-up' of an ancient pagan symbol and the work of local monks from Missenden Abbey. Scouring (or cleaning the exposed area of the cross) was a festive custom. A report, written a few decades before this photograph was taken, records that the scouring 'is borne by the neighbourhood and never without a merrymaking'. The cross is now scoured with modern weedkillers.

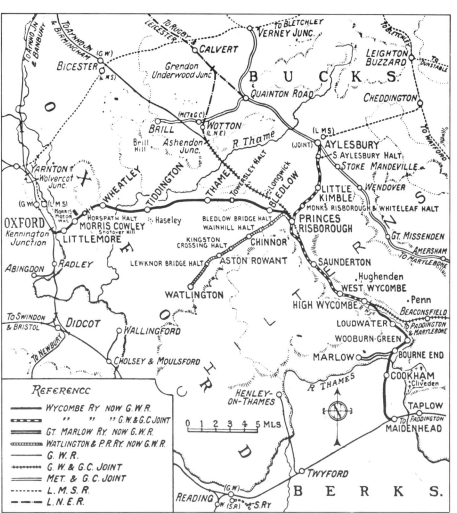

Princes Risborough – multiple rail junction

From the air, the network of lines and sidings formed around Princes Risborough station in the height of its position as a rail junction make a complicated pattern. Six lines run through the station, with an early branch on the right towards Kimble and Aylesbury, and the embanked turn on the left leading towards Oxford and Watlington. Although a line to the Chinnor cement works still exists, the main line is now single-tracked. An early 1930s scene.

Map of the Vale of Aylesbury and its railways c1933 (Top right)

In the map from the *Railway Magazine*, the GW & GC Joint line and its associated railways clearly serve most of the tiny Chiltern communities as well as the major towns. With patience, it was possible to travel anywhere in the Chilterns by train, as the map shows, but in most cases the route lay through Princes Risborough Station.

Princes Risborough

Despite the fact that the town is one of the smaller market centres in the Chilterns, Princes Risborough had one of the busiest stations. Branch trains started out from here to Watlington, Aylesbury and along the line to Thame and Oxford. The North Signal Box had over 100 levers in a frame the length of a cricket pitch! The South Box served the goods yard.

Princes Risborough
Early days: a GWR locomotive with mixed goods train. The old station is seen here about the turn of the century. The GWR had taken over the Maidenhead, Wycombe & Aylesbury Railway on 1 February 1867. The track seen here was one of the earliest sections to be converted to standard gauge, in October 1868. But note that the original spaced sleepers are still used. The wooden houses on the left were later demolished with the 'Railway Tavern'. On the right is the line for the Watlington branch train, which about this date left at 8.20 am, 9.25 am, 1.10 pm, 3.50 pm and 7.30 pm. There was also a goods train to Watlington at 12.15.

The local connection
A damp day at Princes Risborough, which became a multiple junction with the arrival of the GW and GC Joint Line. This 1954 scene shows little activity on the platform as Tank locomotive No. 1442 arrives with the train for Oxford.

Princes Risborough
Busy scene at the end of the steam era. Ex-LNER stock train on left, just arrived from Marylebone; centre train with 0-6-0 Tank engine No. 5424 from Banbury on an all stations, and right, No. 5409 in the Aylesbury bay platform.

Hall passing Princes Risborough
'Hall' Class No. 5900 working a Paddington bound express on 23 July 1951. The station at that time had two through roads. This is a typical mid-50s view, with hardly a soul on the platforms. On the far side, in the leisurely way of branch line trains, a local bound for Watlington waits in the sunshine.

Princes Risborough
There was always some activity at Risborough in steam days. Here is the Watlington train *The Watlington Donkey*. On 25 April 1925 the GWR advertised a special train right from Paddington via Risborough to Watlington so that town types could go bluebell picking (what would the conservationists have said today!) The last train down the single track line past the Chinnor cement works and the foot of the lovely Chilterns to Watlington ran on 29 June 1957. Part of the line as far as Chinnor remains open for cement carrying trains. The auto-trailer is No. 85 – originally a steam rail car of 1908.

Princes Risborough
Local services arriving together at Princes Risborough on 23 July 1955, both with auto-trailers. The train on the left (with No. 1473) is from Banbury, whilst that on the right is from Aylesbury.

Harvesting near Whyteleaf Cross
The new railway brought London very close in time to these farm labourers' sons whose elder brothers had already been drawn to leave the rural life on the land for the lure of better wages and a new life in the big cities. In those flamboyant Edwardian years before the First World War the reaper-binder had already started to mechanise farming methods, just as the great railway age had made travel possible for the labouring people.

This scene is in the fields near Monks Risborough about 1910. The damage to the grass scarp of Whyteleaf Cross behind can be seen clearly near the lower ground – the village boys had a habit of riding down the slope on wood faggots.

Across the Green Desert

FORWARD.

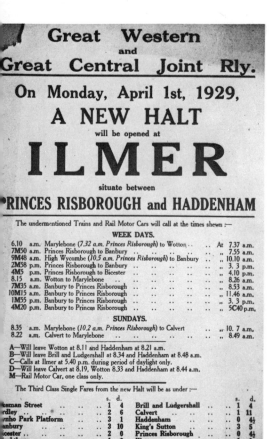

Ilmer halt
Handbill of March 1929 announcing the new halt at Ilmer, a tiny straggle of cottages and farms just off the Risborough-Thame road.

Haddenham
Local train bound for Princes Risborough in 1939, with 0-6-0 No. 4873 and auto-trailer No. 34.

Ilmer
Weeding the fields was hard work before chemicals were used. A farm labourer at work about 1912, with horse and a hand-held hoe, in the Vale of Aylesbury. In spite of the apparent danger of the horse crushing the growing plants, the man-horse team was a very practical farming method.

Haddenham
Beyond Princes Risborough, the Joint Line ran through almost unknown countryside. It was true that this very rural region had already been marked with some miles of railway (the town of Aylesbury had been linked to the London and Birmingham at Cheddington since 1839). There was also the Maidenhead-Wycombe and Aylesbury single track railway of 1854/63, and the line through Thame, but these were local lines. Their main source of revenue was based on the movements of agricultural produce.

A writer in the *Railway Magazine* for November 1899, only a few years before the building of the Joint Line, was able to describe a journey on one of these local lines as resembling 'a country drive . . . now through woodlands, now through fields, pasture-lands and cottage homes' and adding: 'the district is such that the average pleasure seeker is not tempted to while away his time therein'.

Haddenham was the first village beyond Princes Risborough. It was a village whose only claims to fame were the quality of its Aylesbury ducks and the unusual local custom of building thatched walls out of local clay. This tightly-knit community was mocked by neighbouring villages as 'Silly Haddenham who thatched the ponds to keep the ducks dry', a doggerel referring to the walls around the village pond. The arrival of the new railway barely affected life here, or caused any village expansion.

North westwards came another junction at Ashendon, where the Great Central Railway branched away to the hamlet of Wotton. The station known as Brill and Ludgershall on the main GWR line was a long way from either of these little villages.

Brill was, in a vague way, already linked with London by the Metropolitan Railway's curious little tramway running to Quinton Road. A Mr Goodman of the Great Northern

Haddenham

Two views of this large village. The upper photograph shows a scene of about 1908 with almost the whole population in the village street. The new railway from London had just reached this large village on the Oxfordshire border. The picture shows a village with no real pavement, and the usual Victorian wash of horse-dung and muddy water that made crossing the road such an unpleasant experience.

In the shop on the left is what may have been the general stores (Charlie Inc) plus the adjacent inn. The most interesting thing is perhaps the thatched wall in the background.

Haddenham was unusual in its layout, with small crofts of land, surrounded by these high walls, known as 'wichert walls'. They once had thatched tops, but are now topped with clay or slate. Wichert is made from special local clay mixed with straw. Many cottages also had this home-spun walling materials, which was prepared in winter and left for the frosts to break down. After being trodden into a dough-like consistency, and with the chopped straw, the mix was pressed down to form walls between two and three feet thick. Haddenham only expanded when the RAF came and built an airfield in the Second World War. The station closed in 1964.

Railway, who ventured out as far as Brill at this time found it 'a quaint little town and boasts a mineral spring as well as old buildings . . . that have a grimy appearance'.

At Wotton, an elderly lady who was born in a cottage beside the station told us as we researched this book: 'I was here when they built the railway, and I am still here now they've taken it away – it's made no difference in my life.'

The main Great Western line linked up at Bicester (which had another station on the old LNWR line from Bletchley to Oxford). Beyond, the railway cut through the northern outcrops of the Cotswold limestone around Ardley and then joined the old Great Western line from Oxford to Banbury and Birmingham at Aynho.

At King's Sutton, between the junction and Banbury, the line actually runs along the Northamptonshire border for a few miles. King's Sutton, with its very tall church spire, was, oddly enough, at one time a spa of sorts.

At Astrop, half a mile away, John Aubrey had discovered the medicinal quality of the little spring, adding 'I'll not send my patients now as far as Tunbridge'. An observer of the local events in 1749 noted that the waters 'hath enriched a poor obscure village'. But long before the railways were built here, King's Sutton had lapsed back into slumber again.

Ashendon Junction *(Top left)*
Marylebone express coming under the GWR 'up' line with A3 Class engine *Sir Frederick Banbury*.

Ashendon Junction *(Middle left)*
A Manchester to Marylebone express passing under the GWR 'up' line with LNER V2 Class locomotive No. 60862 on 27 August 1955.

Ashendon Junction *(Lower left)*
Paddington express with No. 6014 *King Henry VII* in August 1955. The locomotive was withdrawn in September 1962.

Wotton station (Great Central) *(Top right)*
With the arrival of the direct Great Central services to Marylebone in November 1905, a fast direct connection with London was established, and the tiny rural traffic was quickly drawn away from the earlier station, only 100 yards away, of the Brill Tramway whose train was subject to a speed limit of 8 mph at crossings (although permission was given in 1911 for the Tramway locomotives to run at 25 mph on normal sections!) The GC, which had exclusive rights over the section to Ashendon Junction, carried out bold advertising; the imaginative posters in this picture announce fast express services to the docks, goods traffic facilities between London and Manchester, the quad-royal size poster boldly proclaiming the Great Central's new Suburban train service from 2 April. The horses are with a carriage awaiting the arrival of guests for nearby Wotton House.

Some early morning trains for Marylebone started from Wotton station in the 1920s.

The station closed on 7 December 1953.

Wotton station (Metropolitan Railway) *(Lower right)*
This view of Wotton station on the old Wotton Tramway and later the Brill branch of the Metropolitan Railway, was taken by S.W.A. Newton during the construction of the Great Central's spur line from Ashendon Junction to Grendon Underwood Junction which linked the Great Central main line with the new Joint GC & GW Line. An easement over the Tramway was granted to the GW & GC Joint Committee in April 1903. The Great Central opened its own station at Wotton in November 1905, and in later years the two stations were handled by a Joint station master. The Brill Tramway, which was worked by a Joint Committee of the Metropolitan and Great Central railway from 2 April 1906, experienced a flurry of traffic during the construction of the Great Central spur line from contractors' materials. It showed an unusual profit of £693 for the year ending June 1904.

This view shows clearly the main track, which was relaid by the Joint Committee because of its poor state, the goods siding and the siding in the foreground which lead to a stable. Beyond the station building with its waiting room, booking office and toilets, was another spur line leading to a cattle dock.

Brill & Ludgershall

A group of guns: Guests at a country house near Brill turn out for a Sunday morning shoot, with their dogs. These Edwardian guests have arrived on a Friday afternoon at Brill & Ludgershall station and have been met by horse and trap or even an early motor car for their country weekend, marked with the consumption of prodigious amounts of food and drink.

Brill & Ludgershall

What delights there were for the photographer in the summer of 1935 along the 'Bicester' cut off line! This local train with its 0-6-0 Tank engine No. 5419 and auto-trailer No. 53 is bound for Risborough, but it is unlikely that there are many passengers sitting in the dusty and rather smelly old saloon.

Brill & Ludgershall

Rural peace on a warm afternoon one summer between the World Wars until a Birmingham train rumbles along towards Brill tunnel with an unidentified locomotive and one of the old clerestory coaches. The Metropolitan's Brill branch line crossed over the GWR near the tunnel.

The Grand Pavilion, Brill

In the woods between the villages of Dorton and Brill flows a mineral spring that was exploited in early Victorian times to obtain spa waters of medicinal worth. It was hoped to secure the favours of the young Queen Victoria to build Brill into a fashionable spa town, and an imposing building mushroomed in the deep Buckinghamshire countryside. The Queen chose Leamington, and Brill Spa collapsed into oblivion. However, even in the early 1930s, an over-enthusiastic writer in the *Great Western Magazine* was urging the history seeker to go to Brill & Ludgershall station, and set out for a very long trudge to the remains of Brill Spa, at that time encapsulated as a small well covered with heavy wooden boards and a lock to prevent drunken excesses.

Brill & Ludgershall

Wood Siding – this is a well-known shot of a London Transport train at the halt at Wood Siding shortly before closure of the Brill branch line from Quainton Road in 1935. The steelwork carrying this fascinating branch over the GWR main line can be seen in the foreground, and remained in position for many years after the Second World War, being crossed by the authors in 1966.

The Bicester "Slip"
An historic picture taken at 6.12 pm on 9 September 1960, of the very last slip-coach operation carried out in Britain. The slip carriage is Number 7374, converted for this work as late as 1958.

Bicester
Light and shadow: the afternoon sun casts strong shadows on the huddle of ancient buildings in the main square. The population is absent, except for one small boy in this 1910 picture. Here is a Bicester unspoiled by heavy traffic, military camps and commercial buildings.

Bicester

It is the summer of 1957 and a Paddington express is passing non-stop with a modified 'Hall' Class locomotive *Witherstock Hall*. This engine ran until December 1965 and has now been restored and is used on the Great Central Main Line Steam Trust at Loughborough.

Bicester North signal box

When this picture was taken on 24 October 1961, this box controlled a busy section of track, including sidings. The hanging oil lamp dates from the opening years of the 'Bicester' cut-off section of the new line.

The Village Blacksmith, 1905
A country forge: the Joint Line ran through some of the most popular hunting countryside in the south of England and local hunts were often swelled by visitors, who brought their own horses by the new railway. This rather large forge was owned by the Lewson Brothers, and has trade from the local gentry (notice how this well-to-do gentleman poses for the camera self-consciously while the smith works on the horse) and from repairs to farm machinery, such as the horse-drawn hoe behind the boys.

Bicester
The old 'up' platform on the right, now only used about once a day when diesel car sets have to pass. In the high days of steam Bicester was not well served by express trains. Here *Eydon Hall* is working a through train to London in July 1955. The fir trees in the background are still a feature of the line and appear to have been planted as a decorative feature when the railway was built.

Ardley station

A picture when opening day was not more than a month away. The contractors, Scott and Middleton, have still got the platforms to surface. A train, with building materials is entering the platform on the left, 'wrong road'. The hut on the waggon is awaiting installation just up the line as the cover for a well and pump.

Aynho Park

All seems quiet between trains on a sunny day in 1932. There were two stations serving Aynho and its great house. The older station was on the Oxford-Banbury line nearby and was called 'Aynho for Deddington'. Aynho Park opened on 1 July 1910 as 'Aynho Platform' and lasted until 7 January 1963. The tiny brick booking office still exists (as a store place) on the road beneath the line.

The original route to Banbury from Oxford opened with an official train puffing along, full of dignitaries heading for a 'cold colation' at Leamington. They had the celebrated GWR locomotive *Lord of the Isles* pulling them along. Suddenly, with a frightening jolt, their train ran into another just by Aynho and Deddington station. *Lord of the Isles* fell off the line and by the time they all arrived hours late in Leamington the lunch really was cold.

King's Sutton

The station at King's Sutton opened in 1872 and at one time this attractive village with its very tall church spire had illusions of becoming a spa. The spring of mineral water was situated near the railway within a railed enclosure. The waters were said to have taste equal to Leamington's. The station was also the junction for the line through Chipping Norton and the Cotswolds to Cheltenham.

The locomotive in this pre First World War shot is *La France*, one of several engines built in France for the GWR. *La France* was to inspire the wheel arrangement and design of the famous 'Star' Class on the GWR. The train here is on its way from sunny Bournemouth to murky Birkenhead.

Aynho Junction

The line on the far left is the 'up' track to Bicester and Wycombe, the centre lines go to Oxford and the track on the far right is the 'down' line from Bicester.

Western Diesels *(Opposite)*

Scene in Harbury Cutting between Banbury and Leamington at the end of February 1963 – and a very hard winter. The 8.55 am Birkenhead to Paddington is double headed by D1036 *Western Emperor* and D1040 *Western Queen*.

The 2700PH 'Western' locomotives took over duties from the 'Castles' and 'Kings' in these years and were for the next decade a familiar sight. Their introduction was seen as a great step forward.

Banbury and Beyond

FORWARD.

Banbury
Getting ready to leave for Paddington is 'Castle' Class locomotive *North Star* on 16 March 1952. This engine had an interesting history. Built in 1906 she began life as the GWR's pioneer 4-4-2 four cylinder locomotive, was rebuilt in 1909 as a 4-6-0 and became the first of the 'Star' class, only to be rebuilt yet again in November 1929 as a 'Castle' Class engine. She ended her days in 1957. The carriages on the right are probably for the Hook Norton-Cheltenham service.

Banbury
This old print shows what is stated to be the first train on the new line to Bicester in July 1910. The train is leaving from the bay platform usually reserved for the rail motor train to Hook Norton. The locomotive is one of the GWR's old '517' Class, one of a series of locomotives built at Wolverhampton (1868-1885) and frequently seen on local runs in the Banbury and Birmingham areas until about 1932. Whether this train really is the first through train to Bicester can be questioned. True, the local photographer is on the left and a crew member is making some adjustments to the engine. But are they really awaiting the first through train down from Birmingham?

Banbury *(right)*
Walking up from the GWR station through the town, we find historic Parsons Street. The picture dates from around 1920, but apart from the fashions and the motor car the place had changed little for many years. On the left is 'The Reindeer', a 16th-century inn noted for Hook Norton ales. The brewery exported its potent products via the Cheltenham and Banbury Railway, which joined the GWR at King's Sutton. The original Banbury cake shop (along on the right) was demolished in 1968, but one can still buy both cakes and 'Hooky' ale in Banbury.

Banbury

The GWR was getting up to some exciting things by the latter part of the 1930s and if you passed through Banbury, the chances were that you would have seen this diesel rail-car used on the service to Chipping Norton, No. 14 was built by the Gloucester Carriage and Waggon Company in 1936. The side panels had been removed by 1950, when this picture was taken in the Banbury yard.

Leamington Spa *(top, right)*
New station for old: The first GWR station dated from 1852, when Brunel's Broad Gauge line came up from Oxford and Banbury. The LNWR station had been opened in 1851, with the line from Rugby. Before that, visitors who came to sample Dr Jephson's spa waters had to travel by stage coach from the stations at Coventry or Rugby on the London and Birmingham. The GWR station replaced elegant Eastnor Terrace and the Royal Hotel, an establishment which was '140 yards long and 4 storeys high'. Here workmen are erecting the new steelwork supplied by Jordan and Sons of Newport (Mon) for the rebuilt station of the late 1930s. The 'up' platform was lengthened to 650ft and the 'down' to 670ft. In the background can be seen the LMS tracks.

Leamington Spa
The new station at Leamington Spa in the first weeks of the Second World War. The station buildings are in typical 'modern' Great Western style. The car already has headlight defusers to help with black-out regulations, but is still without the white 'mudguard' patches, so reminiscent of the war scenes. *(lower right)*

Banbury *(above)*
By the 1950s old Banbury station was in a sorry state. Its Brunel overall roof had gone, and the ancient wooden buildings were falling down. Under the footbridge you can see some carriages in the bay platform used for the GCR/LNER trains on the line down from Woodford. The station was rebuilt in concrete and yellow brick in the 1950s – one of the first British Railways new stations, it now provides fairly lavish facilities for what is only a medium size town.

Banbury
'Hall' Class No. 4917 *Crosswood Hall* standing in the yard at Banbury Depot on a fine day in June 1959. The depot supplied locomotives to haul the heavy iron ore trains from the local mine sites, such as those as Astrop just south of the station.

Fenny Compton
This lonely station was near the point where the LMS line from the Midlands crossed the GWR. This rather round-about route opened in July 1871 and soon earned the title 'Slow and Muddle Junction' because of its erratic train running! After its closure on 7 August 1952, the line survived in part for ironstone traffic and army trains and the present junction with the Banbury-Leamington line was built in 1960.

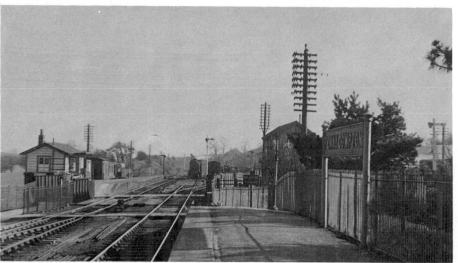

Warwick

Not all trains on the Birmingham line were GWR. Certainly until the late 1950s there was a variety of 'foreign' workings. In this 1928 view, GWR's 'Star' Class locomotive *Dog Star* is taking a return seaside train from the South towards the Midlands, composed of SECR 'bird cage' stock. *Dog Star*, No. 4001, was the first GWR 4-cylinder 4-6-0 and was built at Swindon in February 1907 and withdrawn in January 1934.

Climbing Hatton Bank

After Leamington and Warwick stations, the railway to Birmingham passes through some hilly countryside and climbs the 3¼ miles of 1 in 110 gradient of Hatton Bank. 'Castle' Class No. 5026 *Criccieth Castle* heads a summer Saturday holiday train returning from the sunny south on 22 August 1964.

Hatton
Moor Street, Birmingham commuter train in May 1957 with ex-GWR engine No. 5185.

Lapworth
A Queen in a hurry! Picking up water at speed is 'Star' Class No. 4037 *Queen Philippa* in 1929 as she heads towards Birmingham. Built in December 1910, she was withdrawn in June 1926 and converted at Swindon into a 'Castle' Class locomotive. In March 1937 she was renamed *The South Wales Borderers* and ran until September 1962.

Lapworth
Passing over Rewington troughs in the late 1920s is De Glehn type locomotive *Alliance*, No. 4. She was one of three locomotives the GWR had built in France in 1905. *Alliance* was based on a type of engine used on the Paris-Orleans Railway and she later became the inspiration for the famous 'Stars', 'Castles' and 'Kings'.

Knowle & Dorridge
Two views of a typical GWR Birmingham suburban station. The top view dates from 31 May 1934 and one of the posters advertises excursions to Aberystwith via Snow Hill.

The lower shot shows 'Castle' Class No. 5032 *Usk Castle* with the 11.45 am Birkenhead to Paddington express passing through on 7 September 1957. This locomotive was built in May 1934 and ran until September 1962.

Solihull
Birmingham's built up area begins at Solihull. Here a Class 8100 locomotive pulls out with a Birmingham commuter train on 21 April 1947.

Busy day at Acocks Green, 1932
You didn't have to wait long for local transport in the early 1930s at Acocks Green. With frequent trains to Moor Street, local buses or trams, one could enjoy the delights of the Bull Ring Market and Corporation Street for a few pence. Birmingham's tram fleet was said to be the largest in the world and for many inner city dwellers the way to the city centre was by tram rather than GWR train. The last tram ran on 4th July 1953. Bus services were also very extensive and Birmingham was the first place to adopt closed top buses in 1923.

Tyseley

The GWR sheds here were always a delight for spotters and there seems to have been no restrictions in 1955 when this picture of a 2800 Class locomotive was taken. The other Tyseley picture shows one of the ROD type locomotives built for service in the First World War and purchased by the GWR in 1919. This locomotive ran until May 1956. In the background, an 0-6-0 shunts on the lines beside the main running tracks. *(opposite)*

Birmingham (Moor Street)

In order to relieve pressure on Snow Hill, Moor Street terminus was opened on 1 January 1909 for suburban trains from Leamington and the North Warwickshire lines. The present station buildings date from 1914.

The train on the left is bound for Henley-in-Arden and that on the right for Leamington. A June 1957 view.

Great Western Hotel
The hotel, opened in 1863 set new standards in the then quickly growing city of Birmingham. Enlarged in 1871 with the new station, the building was a landmark in Colmore Row until its demolition is October 1969. During the Second World War the building was seriously damaged in an air raid on 19/20 November 1940 and never regained its old status. On the left, in this Edwardian view, a tramcar is coming up the slope of Snow Hill. The track here originally had a central 'slot' with a cable for propelling the tram cars to the New Inn at Handsworth.

The last train has gone
No more greetings, the happy holiday
crowds, the uniforms of wartime; the school
parties, the businessmen and the
commuters; no more whistles of engines and
the gleam of the sun on brown and cream
carriages and green locomotives. The last
express trains left Snow Hill on Sunday 5
March 1967. The final local services came
to an end on 4 March 1972. Now all that is
left is weeds, dust, rust and the memories of
a railway that was once the last link in the
story of Britain's steam railways.

Credits

Author's Collection
7, 11, 12, 12, 27(T), 37, 54(T), 55, 56, 62, 64(T), 70, 71(T), 72(T & B), 74, 75, 77(B), 82(T), 84, 85(T), 86(T), 88, 97(T), 98(T), 103, 104, 109(T), 111, 112(T & B), 114(B), 121, 123(T & B), 124(T), 125, 127(B), 129(B), 134(T), 136(T), 137(M & B), 139(M & B).

London Borough of Brent (Wembley History Soc. Grange Museum)
20, 53, 56(T).

Buckinghamshire Libraries, High Wycombe
26, 27, 104, 105.

Aylesbury Museum
29(B), 108(B), 118(B).

H.C. Casserley
60, 61(B), 117(B), 118, 120(M), 124(M & B), 134(B).

C.R.L. Coles
48, 51, 57, 58, 59, 61(T), 64(B), 68, 69, 73(T), 76, 78(B), 80, 81, 83, 84(B), 86, 93(B), 96, 114(T), 116(B), 117(T), 138(T).

Miss K. Day
18, 93(T), 97(B), 118(B).

A Fleming
44, 46, 67, 84(T), 90, 91, 95, 98(B), 99, 106, 107(T), 108, 110(B), 112(B), 113, 127(T), 128(B), 132(T), 134(M), 137(T), 139(T), 140(M & T).

London Borough of Ealing
62(B), 63, 66.

William Fenton
19, 21(B), 32, 33, 34, 38, 39, 42, 43, 117(T).

Pat Gadd
34, 49, 120(B).

Helen Hoare Collection
78(T).

London Borough of Hillingdon
71, 79(T & B), 78(M), 82(B), 90(B).

D.A.C. Harrison
137(B).

Illustrated London News
54(B).

London Transport
65, 105(T), 125(B).

Leicestershire Museum, Art Galleries and Records Service
14, 14, 16, 19, 21(T), 22, 23, 24, 27, 28, 36, 52, 89, 100, 101, 112, 125(B).

LGPCo/Real Photographs
71(T), 84(T), 129(B), 133(T), 136.

Oxfordshire County Libraries
126(B), 122(B), 133(B).

Oxford Publishing Co.
41, 77(T), 79(M), 92(T), 94, 119, 126(T), 129(T), 130, 135, 138(T), 141(B).

North Herts Museums
35, 110, 128(T).

Pamlin Prints
141(T).

Science Museum, London
25, 31.

Charles E. Lee
115(T), 120(T).

R. Darlaston
140(B).

T. Stephens
102(B).

B. Stephenson
111(B).

S. Creer
112.

M. Pope
87, 91(B), 138.

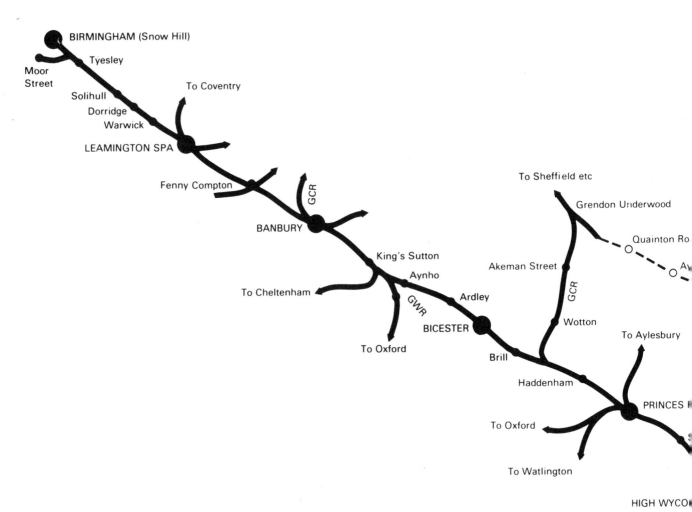

BIRMINGHAM (Snow Hill)

Tyesley

Moor
Street

Solihull

Dorridge

Warwick

LEAMINGTON SPA

To Coventry

Fenny Compton

GCR

BANBURY

King's Sutton

Aynho

To Cheltenham

GWR

Ardley

BICESTER

To Oxford

Brill

Haddenham

To Oxford

To Watlington

To Sheffield etc

Grendon Underwood

Quainton Ro

A

Akeman Street

GCR

Wotton

To Aylesbury

PRINCES

HIGH WYCO

FORWARD

DOMINE·DIRIGE·NOS

VIRTUTE·ET·INDUSTRIA